Horn's Cross on the old Monks' Path, Holne Moor.

In many a green and solemn place + Girt with the wild hills round,
The shadow of the Holy Cross + Yet sleepeth on the ground.

Richard John King (1820-1876)
The Forest of the Dartmoors

DARTMOOR CROSSES

AND SOME ANCIENT TRACKS

F.H. (Harry) Starkey

REVISED EDITION

First published in 1983
by
F.H. Starkey
Second (revised) edition, 1989

Printed in Great Britain by
A. Wheaton & Co. Ltd., Exeter

ISBN 0 950 7240-6-8

To the many Dartmoor lovers, both living and
deceased, whose written works and spoken words have
provided me with so much of the information contained in
this book. Also my friends at Devon Books, my grateful
thanks for their valued help and advice in the
preparation of this revised edition.

Foreword

The purpose of this book is to give people who are interested in the history, folklore and topographical features of Dartmoor as much information as is currently available about the many stone crosses to be found on and around the Moor. Because many of these crosses are associated with, and act as waymarks along, the ancient tracks which traverse the Moor, some information is given about a few of the tracks themselves. Other items of interest are also briefly referred to.

When I first fell in love with Dartmoor many years ago, one of the aspects of the Moor which fascinated me was the fact that everywhere I went, whether on the open moor, in the lanes around the Moor or in the border villages, I found stone crosses. Very many of these were clearly ancient, most of them made from the native granite and the majority of rude construction. I noticed too that a large number of these crosses had been damaged in the past, some probably by accident, some by vandalism and some — all too many in fact — by being adapted for other purposes. The shaft of a granite cross makes a useful gatepost, or lintel or doorstep, especially if the arms are knocked off first. To all these uses, and others, Dartmoor's crosses have been pressed in the past. But for the past century or so enlightenment as to the importance and value of our archaeological heritage has been spreading, with the result that many ancient objects have been recognised and restored. This is as true of Dartmoor and Dartmoor's crosses as elsewhere and to-day a large number of crosses which at the turn of the century were missing or misplaced have been recovered and re-erected for our pleasure and education.

However, despite the splendid work that has been done by dedicated archaeologists and antiquaries, much remains still to do. The fact is that the period of neglect extended over several centuries, beginning with the religious controversies of the 16th and 17th centuries and tapering off in the late 19th century after a long period during which sheer ignorance and lack of interest took over from religious bigotry and intolerance. The result of this is that there are still discoveries to be made. Only this Spring (1982) we have found two badly mutilated octagonal granite shafts, in

5

different parts of Dartmoor, each doing duty as a gatepost at a now disused gateway. These cannot be proved to be the shafts of crosses though it seems likely that they were, but it is important that such discoveries be recorded and reported. If they are not, a subsequent discovery nearby, say a socket-stone or part of the head of a cross, may not be accorded its true significance. I recommend my readers to do as I do — scrutinise every likely stone, be it gatepost or door-step or what you will. At the worst you will be mistaken for some harmless eccentric; at best you may discover some long lost archaeological feature of great importance. If you do find something of interest please let someone in authority know. On Dartmoor the National Park officials are always helpful; elsewhere the curator of the local museum is as good a person as any to pass on the information.

The authorship of a book such as this involves much research into written sources and much investigation on the ground. I have been particularly fortunate in having had access to and encouragement from one who was, in my opinion the foremost authority on the subject of the ancient stone crosses of Devon. I refer of course to Mr. E.N. Masson Phillips, whose ten papers on the subject, published over a period of 50 years in the *Transactions of the Devonshire Association* have been my constant work of reference. In this context I must also mention my friend, Mr. John V. Somers Cocks.

John is a mine of information about historical matters relative to Dartmoor. I have been asking him questions about Dartmoor crosses and other such matters for nearly 25 years now and he never lets me down. He may not know the answer to every question but he can always quote a useful reference — which is just as good.

I have also received much help in practical ways from other friends, May Meredew, Grace and Les Landon, and my son John Starkey among them, and I thank them all. Without their help the writing of this book would have been hard labour rather than a labour of love.

Contents

List of Illustrations

All the line illustrations in this book are from original drawings by John H.A. Starkey.

The cover illustrations and those on pages 76, 82, 94, 145, 146, 149, 151, 152, 154, 159, 166, 168, 173, 174 are from transparencies taken by the author.

Chapter 1

Introduction

The stone crosses to be found on and around Dartmoor fall into a variety of different categories and are of varying age. They are mostly made from granite and for this reason, granite being a somewhat intractable stone, they are, in the main, rather rude as to construction.

The crosses dealt with in this book fall into the following categories:

1. **Village Crosses:** i.e. crosses found occupying a position actually in a village, often but not always near the church. These are usually rather more carefully constructed than the majority of Dartmoor crosses. They are mostly of medieval date and were probably erected to mark a preaching station before the parish church was built. In later years, when the church had taken over the function of the preaching cross, the Village Cross became the secular centre of the village, and here proclamations were made and meetings held.

2. **Churchyard Crosses:** these will be found in the churchyard itself, often occupying a position near the south door. They are usually carefully sculpted and were probably erected to sanctify the church enclosure before the Church itself was built. Later, some Churchyard Crosses became known as Palm Crosses and from them traditional church processions, e.g. on Palm Sunday and Rogation Day, set out. Many existing Churchyard Crosses are clearly medieval in origin and may well be replacements for much earlier crosses dating back to the original church. Today there are several cases where a cross now stands in a churchyard but is not the Churchyard Cross, it having been placed there for safety and convenience. Such cases are noted in the text.

3. **Boundary Crosses:** there are several cases on Dartmoor of crosses marking boundaries but whether they were actually set up as boundary stones it is difficult if not impossible to say. That this was done elsewhere is beyond dispute; the cross gave

potent protection to a boundary in more superstitious days. A notable Dartmoor example is provided by the four crosses which marked the boundary of the Manor of Brent. This is dealt with fully in a later chapter.

4. **Wayside Crosses:** these provide by far the greater proportion of Dartmoor crosses. They stand along the ancient tracks which traverse the Moor, along lanes and at the intersections of lanes and tracks. Their purpose was, beyond a doubt, to guide the wayfarer and to assure him that he was on the right track whilst reminding him that he was still under the protection of the Almighty. Who erected them? Who can say? This was the kind of good work sponsored and encouraged by the monks whose monasteries were at that time the terminal points of the tracks along which stood the crosses. The monks encouraged others to provide such facilities, and many a bridge and doubtless many a wayside cross owes its origins to the indulgences granted to the donor by the superior clergy.

5. **Memorial and other miscellaneous crosses;** apart from Childe's Tomb, which is a special case and dealt with at length in a later chapter, there are on and around Dartmoor a number of crosses which can only be called Memorial crosses. Generally speaking these are not ancient but they do arouse interest and give rise to questions and so they are dealt with in a separate chapter.

The subject of the stone crosses of Dartmoor has not been neglected in the past but there have been long gaps between publications and almost everything published on the subject is long out of print. A short bibliography appears at the end of this book but for the reader who is interested in this aspect of the subject here is a brief history of publications.

1876: G.W. Ormerod, a notable antiquary, of Teignmouth, privately published a little book of 69 pages entitled *"Archaeological Memoirs relating to the East of Dartmoor"*. This contains information about existing stone crosses in the vicinity of Chagford, Moretonhampstead, Bovey Tracey, etc.

William Crossing, author of the *"Guide to Dartmoor"*, published in turn

1884: (1) *"The Ancient Crosses of Dartmoor with a description of their Surroundings".*

1892: (2) *"The Old Stone Crosses of the Dartmoor Borders".*

1902: (3) *"The Ancient Stone Crosses of Dartmoor and its Borderland."*
Of these the last is by far the most interesting and complete. All three are long out of print. They are collector's items, very scarce and very valuable.

1937 Mr. E. N. Masson Phillips, F.S.A. in the *Transactions of the*
to *Devonshire Association* for 1937 published the first of ten
1979: papers cataloguing and describing the *"Ancient Stone Crosses of Devon."* The crosses described in these papers include all the Dartmoor crosses known to exist at the time of going to press in 1979. This is a most valuable and informative series of papers.

At this point I suppose, the reader is entitled to enquire, "If the subject has been so well covered by previous writers why is it now necessary to produce yet another book about Dartmoor Crosses?". The answer is simple if not immediately apparent to the casual observer. Ormerod's little book, which covered only part of Dartmoor anyway, is long out of print and unobtainable. The same remarks apply to Crossing's three books, as already stated. As to Masson Phillips' great work; this is scattered through eight volumes of the *Transactions of the Devonshire Association* between 1937 and 1979. It has never been collated and it deals with Devon at large and not just Dartmoor. Generally speaking only members of the Association have these volumes and few of them have complete runs. This means that the enquirer must have recourse to the reference shelves in public libraries, a time-consuming and inconvenient business for the majority of people.

Further, none of these works are now up to date. New discoveries are constantly being made, and I myself have provided Mr Masson Phillips with five items of information for inclusion in his next supplementary paper. No doubt this book will be partly out of date before it is published — such is the nature of archaeology.

But quite apart from any value the book may have as being the most up to date in its particular field, I recommend it to my readers as a pleasant and convenient peg to hang an exploration of Dartmoor on. This is how I started to explore the Moor 30 years ago and given my time again I would do the same. By seeking out each cross in turn the reader will at the end have explored a very large part of central, southern and eastern Dartmoor as well as the whole perimeter of the moor. For the fastnesses of northern Dartmoor a different guide will be required — try Crossing!

Clearly, anyone intending to seek out the crosses mentioned in this book, or to identify and perhaps follow some or all of the ancient tracks referred to, will require a serviceable map. In my opinion the best for the purpose is the Ordnance Survey's *Tourist Map of Dartmoor* at a scale of 1 inch to a mile. This covers the whole of Dartmoor and a large area around the perimeter, including the sites of all the crosses mentioned in the book. Most of the crosses mentioned, but not all, are indicated on the map, but very few indeed are referred to by name. For more detailed exploration the Ordnance Survey's 1:25000 Second Series maps at a scale of about 2½ inches to a mile are ideal, but expensive.

The dating of stone crosses such as we find on Dartmoor and in the border lanes and villages is a matter of considerable difficulty. Some assistance in this is given by the style of an individual cross and the amount of weathering that a particular specimen has undergone, but such considerations as this are very variable and unreliable. I know of one Dartmoor cross which has all the appearance of a 14th or 15th century cross but which I know for certain was not made and erected until the late 1920's or early 30's. The only really reliable evidence as to age is afforded by ancient documents. Unfortunately, these rarely contain any reference to Dartmoor crosses, with one or two notable exceptions which are dealt with later.

However, much thought has been given by experts to the dating of the ancient crosses of Devon and the general concensus at the present time seems to be that, whilst one or two Dartmoor crosses may be of late Saxon date, the majority are probably medieval. It should be noted that very few public crosses were erected during the three centuries that elapsed between the Dissolution of the Monasteries and the beginning of the reign of Queen Victoria in 1837.

Reference has already been made to the fact that many of the crosses we are considering were erected because of the influence of the Christian Church, whose symbol was the cross. These were the days of an almost totally unlettered and vastly superstitious population and it was necessary for the Church to have a symbol which it could present to the common man as being all powerful, guarding him from all dangers and which he could rely upon to ward off all evils. Thinking of Dartmoor in particular it should also be remembered that there were still standing along its many paths and tracks numerous upright stones, relics of the prehistoric people who once lived upon the Moor. Many of these stones had doubtless been used as waymarks by many generations of Devonians. When the new religion swept the country it was easy, and politic, for the old stones to be re-shaped into the likeness of the Cross. There is of course no positive proof that this was done in any particular case but there are several Dartmoor crosses which readily lend themselves to this theory.

If the shaping of old waymarks into new crosses was actually carried out, it probably first happened in Saxon times and may have continued intermittently for centuries. It is interesting to note however that the cross as a symbol has a history older than that of Christianity.

For example, we are told that in Egypt in pre-Christian times the looped cross or Ankh was regarded as a token of immortality. Also, that the cross with equal arms and the fylfot or swastika are both occasionally found in prehistoric contexts. We learn too that the Spanish colonizers of South America were astonished to find that the South American peoples venerated the swastika (which is only a cross with crooked arms) as a symbol of the god of rain.

The use of the cross as the principal symbol of the Christian faith is too well known to need emphasis, but it may be pertinent to point out that the importance of the cross in this connection springs from its use as an implement in the execution of Christ. It is evident that this was no new thing even in those far off days. It is said that Maleus, a General in the army of Carthage, caused his son to be crucified, dressed in royal raiment, as a sacrifice to Baal in return for an expected favour. It seems too that the Romans reserved crucifixion as a punishment for slaves and offenders of the lowest class.

The earliest use of the cross for monumental purposes that I have been able to trace dates from the year 312 AD when the Emperor,

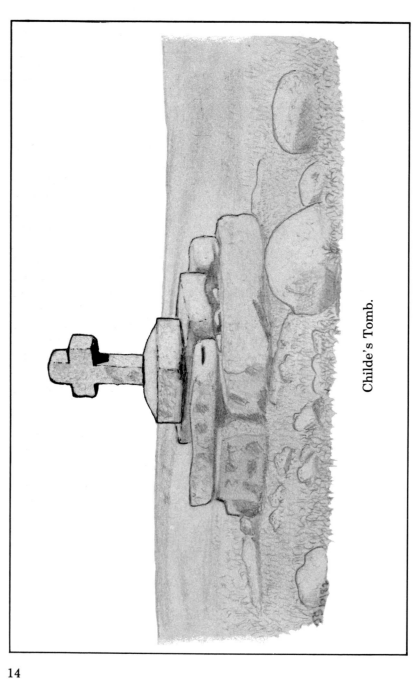

Childe's Tomb.

Constantine the Great, caused crosses to be set up in public places and on public buildings as a thanksgiving for a notable victory by his armies. This followed the alleged appearance in the heavens of the sign of the cross, which was thought to have promised the victory eventually achieved.

The use of the cross to perpetuate the memory of individuals became popular in the late 18th and early 19th centuries and today of course there are tens of thousands of them in our churchyards and cemeteries. But examples of such memorials of earlier date than the 18th century are rare and I know of no genuine Dartmoor example unless Childe's Tomb be one. The cross which stands by the roadside at Sourton Down, not far from Okehampton, bears a memorial inscription dating from Romano-Christian times, but it was a memorial stone before being turned into a cross, probably at a much later date. This cross is fully dealt with in a later chapter.

However, there is a memorial cross, not far from the borders of southern Dartmoor, which may well be of interest and a brief notice of it seems not out of place here. The cross in question is to be found in Stentaway Road, Plymstock, just north of Stentaway House. This cross is of the Celtic type, with a squarish perforated head. It is made from granite and stands something less than five feet tall. For many years it was in use as a rubbing post for cattle in a nearby field and is badly mutilated, having lost a considerable portion of its head. It was moved to its present position in 1946 following representations made by Mr E.N. Masson Phillips, the cost being borne by the Old Plymouth Society. The cross bears an inscription, in characters 4 to 5 inches high, which puzzled scholars for many years. The inscription has now been translated as reading "ELEW" The first three of these characters are Anglo-Saxon capitals and the last is a runic symbol for W and also stands for WYN. Thus the inscription is read as ELEWYN or Aelfwynn. This translation was achieved in 1965 by Miss Elisabeth Barty of Newnham College, Cambridge and is reported by Mr Masson Phillips in T.D.A. Vol. 111 (1979). Mr Masson Phillips points out that the epigraphy of this inscription is of the 10th—11th century and adds that in the late 10th century there was an Aelfwynn, who was the wife of Ordulf (or Ordulph), the founder of Tavistock Abbey which held land at Plymstock. He thinks that the cross was probably a memorial monument. We shall meet another Ordulf, the grandson of the one mentioned above, when we visit Childe's Tomb below Fox Tor on central Dartmoor.

It is a far cry indeed from ancient Rome to the moors and lanes of Dartmoor, but not so far from Plymstock or from Saxon England. This brief resume of the manner in which the cross was used as a symbol in ancient times may serve to give the reader some idea of the vast range of interests to be found in the study of almost any aspect of Dartmoor.

Most of the crosses described in this book lie within the boundaries of the Dartmoor National Park. But a few, for example those at Bovey Tracey, lie outside the Park but are nevertheless within what is generally regarded as being Dartmoor country.

Chapter 2

Crosses marking tracks or paths, or standing along roads or lanes, or at cross-roads.

Crosses falling into this category constitute by far the largest proportion of stone crosses to be found on or around Dartmoor. Before describing the crosses themselves and their location it is necessary to say something about the tracks with which they are associated.

In his *Guide to Dartmoor,* first published in 1909 and happily still in print, William Crossing describes no less than 81 ancient paths and tracks traversing the Moor or connecting different parts of it. In the case of many of these tracks Crossing was the first writer to refer to them, let alone describe them.

Buckfast to Tavistock and Buckland — The Abbots' Way

The first track mentioned in Crossing's list and the most widely known, even to-day, is the ancient route known as and marked on every map as The Abbots' Way. This reputedly connected Buckfast Abbey on the southern side of the Moor with Buckland Abbey on the western side, with a branch going off to Tavistock Abbey, also on the western side. The track started at Buckfast and to-day runs through lanes in a north-westerly direction for about 2½ miles until it reaches a piece of detached common, where five lanes meet, at a spot called Cross Furzes. Here the track descends into the valley of the Dean Burn and after running through enclosures for about a mile enters upon the open moor at Water Oak Corner. The track now runs westward to Huntingdon Cross (about which more later) where it crosses the River Avon by means of a ford and soon mounts to the high ground to the south of the river. A little further westward it descends to and crosses the Erme near its source, then again mounting to the high ground it reaches Broad Rock (a notable boundary mark) where the track divides. From Broad Rock the western arm makes its way via the valley of the Langcombe Brook and Plym Steps on the Plym to the great hill known as Eylesbarrow. From here the Abbots' Way, now a well marked track, descends to Burracombe Gate where it becomes a tar-mac road. This runs along the side of Ringmoor Down, passing Sheepstor village and Burrator Lake in the valley below and eventually arrives, in the shape of a muddy lane, at Marchants Cross. From this point the ancient track runs mainly through lanes to Buckland Abbey.

We now return to Broad Rock, which is a natural granite rock lying on the surface of the Moor. The rock marks the boundary between the Forest of Dartmoor and the parish of Cornwood. It bears two inscriptions; one, the letters "B.B." signifying Blachford Bounds, indicates that this is one of the bound marks of the Manor of Blachford (part of the parish of Cornwood). The other inscription is the words "Broad Rock," the name of the bound mark.*

From Broad Rock the track runs for about a mile across sloping ground and then descends to the valley of the Plym. The current Ordnance Survey maps show the Abbots' Way as crossing the Plym at Plym Ford, but there is some doubt about this, some authorities holding that it crosses the river further upstream. However this may be, cross the river it does, and makes its way to Nuns' Cross, close to the abandoned Nuns' Cross Farm, which stands about a mile and a quarter NNW of the river valley. There is a track which by a devious route, connects Plym Ford with Nuns' Cross Farm, but whether this is the original Abbots' Way none can say.

At Nuns' Cross the Abbots' Way meets another track, which coming from the east, also connectes Buckfast Abbey with Buckland Abbey. No official name attaches to this track, but in view of its importance it ought to have one and so I propose to call it The Monks' Path. This track was probably used by the monks to a much greater extent than was the Abbots' Way, and, as there are many ancient crosses along its route, it will be fully dealt with later on.

Meanwhile, back to The Abbots' Way. On leaving Nuns' Cross the track takes a course which is a little west of north and skirts the village of Princetown. It then traverses the hillside below North Hessary Tor and crosses Longash Common to Merrivale Bridge where it crosses the Walkham river; (formerly it crossed at a ford a

---

* An interesting feature of Devon and Dartmoor in particular, is that very many bound marks have individual names, e.g. Broad Rock, Blue Jug, Old Jack and so on.

little below the present bridge). The track now takes to the common again and passing close to Vixen Tor comes by way of the Windypost (a granite cross) to Pixies' Cross on Whitchurch Down. West of Pixies' Cross is another granite cross by the road-side and just to the west of this lies the town of Tavistock, the site of the ancient abbey of the same name.

Before entering upon a description of the crosses mentioned in connection with The Abbots' Way it might be as well to say a word or two about the religious houses with which it is reputed to have been associated. Buckfast Abbey, originally a Benedictine house but later Cistercian (and now again Benedictine) was founded in 1018. Among its endowments was an estate comprising no less than 10,000 acres of Devonshire, much of which lay on or near Dartmoor. Tavistock Abbey also was a Benedictine house; it was founded in 981 by Ordulf, Earl of Devon and under the patronage of the boy King Ethelred. As for Buckland Abbey, it was by far the junior of the three. A Cistercian foundation, it was founded in 1275 and endowed by its benefactor and foundress, Amicia, Countess of Devon, with a vast estate, the gift of her daughter Isabella de Fortibus, Countess of Albemarle.

Earlier authorities seem to have had no doubt about the authenticity of The Abbots' Way, but for many years now there has been some dispute about its provenance. Richard Hansford Worth, one of the most distinguished figures ever to adorn the Dartmoor scene, paid considerable attention to this track. He remarked that the earliest use of the name "Abbots' Way" that he could discover was by a Dartmoor lover named John Andrews, a solicitor of Modbury, about 1790. Prior to this the track was known as the Jobbers' Cawse, the Jobbers being the itinerant dealers in wool who presumably used the track in the course of their journeyings. Worth also points out that a much more reasonable track for the monks to have used between Buckfast and Tavistock or Buckland would have been the one already referred to and dubbed "The Monks' Path". With this contention one must agree.

It is notable that, using the Abbots' Way, the wayfarer encounters only one cross between Cross Furzes and Broad Rock. This is Huntingdon Cross, already mentioned, which stands near the ford over the Avon about 2 miles west of Water Oak Corner. Records exist which show that this cross, with three others, only one of which still exists, was erected about 1550 to mark the

Huntingdon Cross.

boundary of the Manor of Brent. This manor was part of the lands of Buckfast Abbey. After the dissolution in 1539, the manor came into the possession of Sir Thomas Denys and later Sir William Petre and it was the latter's boundaries that are said to have been receiving attention when the cross was erected.

Huntingdon Cross is a rough but quite well shaped cross constructed from granite. It stands about 4½ feet high and measures about 22 inches across the arms. The place where it stands is known as Lower Huntington Corner. Nearby the Western Wella Brook comes coursing down the hillside and just to the north-west stands the great hill, known as Huntingdon Warren, formerly the site of a rabbit farm.

The other three crosses referred to as marking the boundaries of the Manor of Brent stood as follows.

1.   At Buckland Ford, a crossing place on a little brook which falls into the Avon not far upstream from Huntingdon Cross. This cross has not been seen in living memory, and Crossing says that he was unable to find anyone who had seen it.

2.   On a cairn of stones known as Western Whittaburrow, which stands on top of the ridge south of the Avon. This cairn is a Bronze Age burial place and is a landmark for miles around. The cross that stood here was known as Petre's Cross and it was destroyed about 1847 by workmen who built themselves a house on the cairn and having knocked off the arms of the cross built it into the fabric of their building to serve as the clavel over the fireplace. The building was largely demolished years after and the cross was then found. The remains of the building are still visible. The cross was re-erected to serve as a boundary mark and still stands on the cairn with its damaged head buried among the boulders and the tenon at the base of the shaft pointing to the sky. A four foot length of shaft is visible today and a further two feet are buried beneath the stones. I am informed on good authority that recent investigation has shown that both arms are indeed missing; that one arm has been knocked off fairly cleanly but the other has carried away part of the head also, leaving a very badly mutilated cross. The shaft bears a bench mark, presumably cut upon it by the officials of the Ordnance Survey.

3.   On the summit of the hill known as Three Barrows, nearly two

miles south of Western Whittaburrow. The mutilated head of the cross turns up among the mass of boulders on the hilltop from time to time. Its last recorded appearance was in 1957. I have searched for but have never succeeded in finding it.

The question arises whether the four boundary crosses referred to above were made for the purpose or whether they were perhaps filched from elsewhere. It must be remembered that the hand of the image-breaker was hard at work in the mid-16th century and that it is a great deal easier and quicker to remove a granite cross than it is to carve one from the rock. There is at least a suspicion that the cross that used to stand on Three Barrows was formerly known as Hobajohn's Cross and stood at a spot nearly a mile to the south of its last known position. This place is now marked by a pillar of granite with a small cross deeply incised upon it. It seems to mark the boundary line between the parishes of Harford and Ugborough, and is always known as Hobajohn's Cross.

The cross at Buckland Ford and Huntingdon Cross both stood more or less upon the line of the Abbots' Way and would have needed to be moved very little to act as boundary markers. Petre's Cross on Western Whittaburrow is some little distance (about a quarter of a mile) to the south of the Abbots' Way, but here the remarks made about Hobajohn's Cross apply also. On the whole it seems likely that the four boundary crosses were not purpose-made but were merely pressed into service at a time in our history when the cross, as a symbol, had lost much of its sanctity as the result of the Reformation.

As previously stated, the only cross standing upon the reputed route of the western arm of the Abbots' Way, is Marchants' Cross. This stands at the intersection of two lanes a little to the south of Marchants' Bridge just outside the village of Meavy. The lane that runs eastward from this point reputedly follows the line taken by the Abbots' Way. The cross itself is very tall, over eight feet high, and is massively constructed from granite. For many years this cross has borne its present name which is probably a corruption of "Merchants'". Perhaps it and the nearby bridge were the gift of some individual or guild of merchants.

Until the 1940's it was thought by some authorities that Marchants' Cross was originally known as Smalacumbacrosse, otherwise Smallacombe Cross. This was the name of one of the boundary markers named in the deed of gift by which the Countess

Marchants' Cross.

of Devon made over to the monks of Buckland Abbey the lands referred to earlier. (This deed will be discussed at greater length later when Nuns' Cross is dealt with). However, in the *Transactions of the Devonshire Association* for 1942 the late Richard Hansford Worth expressed the opinion that Marchants' Cross was not Smallacombe Cross although he had previously thought that it was. This change of opinion was based upon the fact that the boundary laid down in the ancient deed must have run close to the head of the stream called Smallcombe Lake near Ringmoor Cot, which is nearly a mile to the east of where Marchants' Cross now stands and that the site of Smallacombe Cross would have been in that vicinity.

On another occasion, Worth suggested that a cross now standing near the church in Sheepstor village might be the original Smallacombe Cross. The Sheepstor Cross will be described later on. Meanwhile, the matter is in doubt, but due deference must be given to the opinion of so reputable authority as Hansford Worth. It is of interest to note that Marchants' Cross not only marked the route for travellers along the Abbots' Way but also performed a like service for those journeying between the Augustinian Priory at Plympton and its daughter churches at Meavy and Sampford Spiney and so on to Tavistock. There are other crosses along this route which we shall visit later on.

We now return again to Broad Rock and from there follow the branch of the Abbots' Way which runs roughly north-west and brings us to Plym Ford. This is a convenient crossing place and passable at most times of the year. Having crossed, we continue along the track which at first veers away north-eastward but later turns NW and after about a mile and a half brings us to the edge of the enclosures of Nuns' Cross Farm. This farm is now abandoned but the farmhouse still stands. We skirt the enclosure wall to the west and soon see ahead of us and quite close to the wall a cross—Nuns' Cross itself.

Nuns' Cross is a truly massive monument. Constructed from granite, it stands well over seven feet tall and the shaft, which is rectangular in section, has an average width of 18 inches and an average thickness of about 14 inches. The cross has a rather strange lopsided appearance caused by the fact that the arms, which are short compared with the thickness of the shaft, are of different depths. It will be noticed that the shaft has been broken at some time. Crossing says that this happened in 1846 when the cross was thrown down by two lads. It was repaired and re-erected in the same year. The cross is thought to be of late Saxon or early medieval date.

A careful examination of Nuns' Cross will reveal that it has two inscriptions engraved upon it. On the eastern face, across the arms the word SIWARD appears and on the shaft below the arms on the western side are the words BOC LOND, one above the other. This cross is mentioned in several ancient documents as being a bound mark, either of the Forest of Dartmoor, which lies immediately to the east, or of the lands owned by the monks of Buckland, i.e. the Manor of Walkhampton, which lies to the west of the cross. The dates of the documents concerned with the Forest boundaries are 1240 and 1609 and those with the Buckland Abbey lands 1280 and 1291.

In the ancient documents just mentioned the name of the cross is recorded as Siward's Cross (or in the Latin form *Crucem Sywardi*). The name of this cross gives rise to two puzzles; first as to who Siward (or Syward) was and next how it came to change its name to Nuns' Cross. Neither of these questions has been satisfactorily resolved. It is known that Siward, Earl of Northumberland held extensive estates round Tavistock during the reign of Edward the Confessor before the Norman Conquest. But there is no evidence to connect him with this spot, although Crossing felt that it might have been the case that the Forest of Dartmoor was held by Siward under grant from the Saxon king and that the cross bears his name in consequence. The issue is far from clear however and is made less so by the fact that a family named Siward was settled at Cholwich Town, only a few miles to the south of the cross, as early as the 13th century, though no connection between them and Nuns' Cross can be proved either. Since Tavistock Abbey was founded in the late 10th century and as Nuns' Cross indisputably marks the route across the Moor from Buckfast to Tavistock it is possible also that it was erected as a waymark and later adopted as a boundmark both for the Forest and the Manor of Walkhampton.

The derivation of the name Nuns' Cross is no less uncertain. There is no legend or folk memory associating this place with nuns as far as I have been able to discover. Crossing, however, points out that the word *NANS* in the Cornu-Celtic tongue means a valley or ravine and suggests that *NUNS,* as used here is perhaps a corruption of this word. So it may be, for the cross stands at the head of a valley in which, just to the south-east, rises the Swincombe River, a

Nuns' Cross.

tributary of the West Dart.

The second inscription on the cross, BOC LOND, gives rise to less conjecture. There are probably a dozen places in Devon bearing the name Buckland and about the derivation of this name the authorities seem to have no doubt. It means, they say, Book-land, in other words land held by virtue of a charter or writing. We know that the land whose eastern boundary is marked by this cross was held by the monks of Buckland by virtue of a charter, indeed the very existence of their abbey was founded upon it and it seems certain that the inscription on the cross was intended to record the fact.

Having come along the north-western arm of the Abbots' Way so far, at Nuns' Cross we have also joined the other ancient track, mentioned earlier, which has come from Buckfast Abbey by a different route. At Nuns' Cross this second track divides, one arm going off westward to Buckland Abbey, the other north-westward, making for Tavistock and merging with the Abbots' Way, or vice versa. This is the track referred to earlier as The Monks' Path, a name which has no historical probity but is used here for convenience only. From Nuns' Cross, whether we go to Buckland or Tavistock, we shall encounter several ancient crosses along the route and so, in order to make explanations as clear as possible we shall go first to Tavistock, then return to Buckfast and take the track to Buckland.

The precise route taken by the Abbots' Way/Monks' Path from Nuns' Cross to Merrivale is somewhat uncertain: It is certain however that it passed close to where Princetown now stands and crossed the River Walkham at a ford just below Merrivale Bridge. It is perhaps significant that on Walkhampton Common and Longash Common, west of Princetown, are a number of guide posts. These are posts of granite about 5 feet tall each bearing the letters A on one side and T on the other, indicating the route to Ashburton and Tavistock respectively. It is thought that these posts, and others now missing, were erected towards the end of the 17th century at the expense of local highway authorities. It is known that the Corporation of Plymouth subscribed the sum of £2 for such a purpose in 1699. It is not of course suggested that these posts had any connection with the monks, they and their abbeys had long since disappeared by 1699, but it does seem likely that the 17th century route would have followed the line of the earlier one. It is interesting also to note that east of the Walkham valley there are no stone crosses until one comes to Nuns' Cross, whereas west of the

Walkham there are at least three crosses still surviving (and probably there were formerly others now missing) but no inscribed guide posts as described above.

Having passed by or through Princetown and arrived at Merrivale Bridge we now take to the common and pursue a southwesterly course, keeping Vixen Tor on our left and the rocks of Feather Tor ahead of us. Just before reaching Feather Tor we shall come to a running stream, and by the stream a cross. This is a fine specimen, much more carefully cut than most Dartmoor crosses, with octagonal shaft and arms. It stands seven feet tall and is over two feet across the arms. The everyday name of this cross is the Windypost; stand here in half a gale in January and you will understand its name. But its earlier and more formal name was Beckamoor Cross—the stream by which it stands runs down Beckamoor Combe. The style of this cross is somewhat later than most, but whether it is really as late as the 16th century, as conjectured by Crossing, is somewhat doubtful.

Leaving the Windypost we continue WNW across the common for rather more than a mile. Then, having crossed an unfenced road that traverses the greensward we reach the edge of the golf links on Whitchurch Down. Here, near an old quarry and close to yet another road which runs N-S across the links will be found what must surely be Dartmoor's most rugged cross, Pixies Cross. This stands over seven feet tall and is of massive construction, being about a foot wide with an average thickness of about eleven inches. The arms are uneven in shape and one is slightly higher than the other. The granite from which the cross is made has a decidedly "unfinished" appearance. A small cross is incised between the arms on one side.

With a name like Pixies' Cross one would expect some folk-story about this cross to have survived, and so it has, but not one involving pixies. Instead, the story has a decidedly historical ring about it. It relates that during the period of the Commonwealth, a new vicar came to take charge of Whitchurch parish. He was of the new school and apparently dedicated to Puritan ways of thought and action. These included, of course, an insistence on the destruction of all "images" whose existence were held to pander to idolatry. The items to be destroyed under the new regime included not only crucifixes and statues of the saints, etc., but also wayside crosses. This being so the new vicar's eye soon fell upon Pixies'

Cross and he gave instructions that it was to be removed and destroyed. No-one could be found willing to perform this task however, so, being a determined person, our vicar equipped himself with the necessary tools and set out one day to do the job himself.

He was soon hard at work, but after a while heard a strange noise behind him. On looking round he discovered that he was being addressed by a large and savage bull whose attitude left no doubt as to his intentions. Not being given to running, the vicar took an alternative couse of action and instead shinned up the cross and sat astride the arms, in the hope, one supposes, that the bull would soon tire of a fruitless game and go away.

Not so however, the bull was as determined as the parson, and all through the long hot summer's day the status quo prevailed. When darkness fell, the parson was still up the cross and the bull in attendance and when dawn broke next day they were still there.

With the dawn another party appeared on the scene. This was a little old country-woman, making her way across the common with a basket of butter and eggs for sale in Tavistock market. On approaching the cross she found its familiar outline somehow different, for there, in the dimpsey light and silhouetted against the morning sky was a strange black figure perched upon the cross and a black and sinister four-legged horned creature hovering in attendance. The old lady took in the situation at a glance. She at once recognised the figure sitting on the cross as the Devil and the other creature could only be the great black goat that always accompanied him. Her reaction was immediate and dropping her basket she fled into the nearby village crying that she had just seen the Devil sitting on Pixies' Cross. The villagers were made of sterner stuff apparently and, so it is said, turned out as one man to see what was going on. On arrival of course they found that it was their parson, and not the Devil, who was the cause of all the hullabaloo, for there he sat upon the cross with his tools scattered all around to show the reason for his being there. No doubt someone in the crowd recognised the bull too!

It appears that the vicar was very glad to see his parishioners approaching and being very uncomfortable demanded that they drive the bull away so that he could descend from his perch. But they recognised their advantage and before removing the bull insisted upon the vicar promising not to interfere with the cross in future. He seems to have kept his promise, for the cross is still there and as far as can be seen is undamaged.

It seems likely that the story of the bull and the parson is apocryphal rather than true, but there were some very odd goings on in this part of Devon during Oliver Cromwell's reign and one at least very harsh and overbearing clergyman had charge of Whitchurch Parish during that period.

From Pixies' Cross we join the road that runs westward across Whitchurch Down towards Tavistock and follows it towards the town. About half a mile along, at a point where another road goes off to the left, we find the last surviving cross along the Abbot's Way. This consists of the head and arms of a fair sized cross that has been broken off just below the arms and set up upon a short stumpy shaft that clearly does not belong to the head. This gives the cross a somewhat incongruous appearance, but at least the head has not been lost to us which would probably have been the case if the restoration had not been undertaken. It may be that this cross stands at or near its original position.

From the cross just described it is only about half a mile to the centre of Tavistock where is the site of the ancient abbey for which the wayfarer along the Abbots' Way would probably have been making.

Chapter 3

Buckfast to Buckland — The Monks' Path

We now return to Buckfast Abbey so that we may follow the other ancient track linking it with Tavistock and Buckland Abbeys.

On leaving Buckfast, the first three miles or so of the route lies north-westward through the lanes which bring us at last to the village of Holne. About two miles from Buckfast however we come to our first cross. This stands at a cross-roads where a road goes off to the left (west) to Combe and Cross Furzes. Here stands a venerable tree—Stumpy Oak by name—and under the tree a cross, Hawson Cross. This is a splendid specimen consisting of a massive head and short piece of shaft mounted upon a replacement shaft specially designed for it. The height of the cross is seven feet three inches. The head and short length of the shaft had for many years been built into the hedge nearby. In 1952 the Dartmoor Preservation Association undertook the restoration of the cross. This was achieved with the co-operation of the owner and the assistance of Mr. Masson Phillips, who designed the shaft. It is reasonably certain that Hawson Cross was one of the markers along the Monks' Path and it is quite likely that its present position is at or near its original site.

Passing on through the lanes another mile or thereabouts brings us to the village of Holne. Here, in the churchyard and doing duty as a gravestone, is another ancient cross which will be discussed later on. Meanwhile, we pass through the village, noting the lovely old Church House Inn as we go, and eventually, having negotiated a cattle-grid find ourselves at Holne Moor Gate. Here we leave the road and take to the open moor, following a well marked track that leaves the road just beyond the cattle-grid and takes a westerly course across the common. We are now following the line of the original Monks' Path which itself was taken over and developed by the tinners who worked at the nearby Ringleshutts mine. Soon the track brings us to the Wennaford Brook, which we cross by means of a clapper bridge. Formerly there was a ford here which, tradition has it, was marked by a cross. The cross if it ever existed has long disappeared, but the name of the ford remains—Workman's Ford.

Hawson Cross.

Beyond the ford the track veers away to the left (south) to the long abandoned mine not far away. We maintain our westerly course however and follow the path which is sometimes distinct and sometimes almost indiscernable. About half a mile or so from Workman's Ford, we see a standing cross on the high ground ahead of us—Horns' Cross.

On reaching it we find that this has a rather battered granite head with one broken arm, secured to a disproportionately tall and bulky shaft, clearly a replacement. Crossing tells us that in his day the head alone of the cross lay upon the greensward at this spot. The cross stands in a rough square socket stone which may or may not be original. The date of the restoration of Horns' Cross seems to be unknown at present.

Crossing relates that the ancient name of the place where Horns' Cross stands was Stacombe's Telling-place, from the practice of the farmer at the nearby farm of Staddiscombe, who habitually gathered his sheep here to count them.

The Monks' Path is crossed at Horns' Cross by another old track which connects places in the vicinity of Hexworthy and Dartmeet with South Brent.

From Horns' Cross we continue in a north-westerly direction and soon find that the ground is falling to the west. Having crossed a running stream—the Holne Moor Leat—and a couple of dry channels, we come to the banks of a brook. This is the Wo Brook (or O Brook) and this we must cross, probably by means of the boulders piled up near a washed out ford. By crossing the stream we pass out of the parish of Holne and into the Forest of Dartmoor. If we had time, an exploration of the valley of this little stream would be well repaid, it is certainly one of the most beautiful on Dartmoor. But since we have no time to spare on this occasion we cross and immediately climb the very high bank on the further side. This can be made a little easier if we hunt about a bit and find a sunken track which will take us to the high ground on the western side of the stream. When the ground begins to flatten out a little we shall find that our track joins another and better marked one which sweeps round the hillside from the north-west. Near the spot where the two tracks join we shall find another cross, standing in a cleft in a boulder into which it has been cemented to keep it upright. The shaft of this cross is very short and part of it is obviously missing. The shaft has been broken at some time and repaired by means of an iron clamp. The cross has no regular name but is usually referred to as "the cross near Skir Ford", a crossing place on the stream below. It was missing for many years but was rediscovered in 1884 and was later re-erected at the instance of William Crossing.

From the cross last described we make our way almost due west for about a quarter of a mile and soon see another cross ahead of us, on Down Ridge, which is how it is usually described. This is a substantial granite cross standing about six feet high. The shaft of this one too has been broken and repaired. The repairs were carried out in 1885. William Crossing was present when this was done and when the next two crosses to be described were re-erected on the same occasion.

The path now begins to veer away in a south-westerly direction, skirting the valley of the Wo Brook which lies to the south. The ground here is badly broken with ancient peat ties from which local residents and tin-miners have removed thousands of tons of peat in ages past. There are also several long and deep tinners' gullies.

We are now making for the summit of a hill about a mile to the SW of the cross on Down Ridge—Ter Hill. As we draw nearer, we discern what appears to be a post standing near the summit, black against the skyline. On reaching this is turns out to be another cross, but sited in such a way that the arms are in line with the path and not across it so that it is not easily recognisable at a distance. This is unusual if not unique and is probably the result of thoughtlessness when the cross was re-erected. This cross stands rather less than six feet high (it measured six feet six inches before re-erection in 1885) and it is to all intents and purposes undamaged. It measures two feet two inches across the arms.

About a hundred yards to the west of the cross just described, stands another. This is shorter than the last and has been damaged and repaired by means of an iron clamp. Crossing tells the story of how a farmer at Sherburton in the valley of the Swincombe below Ter Hill took a fancy to this cross at some period in the 19th century and removed it and set it up in his farmyard. The Duchy authorities objected to this however and it was returned and left lying at its original site until it was re-erected in 1885.

Our path now continues along a course a trifle south of west, and the ground soon begins to fall to the SW. Now we see ahead of us and about 400 yards from the last cross, a newtake wall in a somewhat ruinous condition. The path brings us to this wall at a point where a gateway has existed in the past, but the gate has long disappeared leaving a gap. Passing through the gap we find ourselves confronted by a tall and massive cross. The area enclosed by the wall we have just passed through is known as Fox Tor Newtake. The cross is usually referred to as "a cross in Fox Tor Newtake" or as "the cross on Mount Misery" this being the local name for the hill upon which it stands, though the name does not appear on the current 2½ inch O.S. map.

Crossing tells us that in 1878 he found the cross lying on the ground and measured it. It is six feet tall and two feet four inches across the arms. It stands in a rough socket-stone which is five inches deep. One corner of the head of the cross seems to have been broken off, perhaps before the cross was made.

Both Crossing and Masson Phillips record that formerly the head of a second cross was to be seen alongside the one just described. Crossing thinks that it had probably been found by workmen repairing the nearby wall and suggests that it might have been the original head of the cross on Childe's Tomb.

In the limited edition (1902) of Crossing's book *The Ancient Stone Crosses of Dartmoor and its Borderland* there is a photograph believed to be by T.A. Falcon, in which the head of the supposed Childe's Tomb cross is clearly shown propped against the shaft of the cross described as being in 'Fox Tor Newtake'.

Leaving the summit of Mount Misery, we continue the descent of its western side. Near the bottom of the hill we pass close to the scanty ruins of a farm, on our right. These are all that remain of Fox Tor Farm, which was newly taken in from the Forest in the early years of the 19th century at a time when great efforts were being made to cultivate Dartmoor. The farm had a very short life and was then abandoned. Eden Phillpotts made Fox Tor Farm the scene of his novel "The American Prisoner", one of his best Dartmoor stories in my opinion.

Just below the ruined farm we cross over a little stream, a branch of the Swincombe river, using a primitive stone bridge to do so. Note the stones of which this bridge is composed, they consist of a number of long granite shafts, similar to rather thin gateposts. They will feature again in our narrative quite soon.

Having crossed the stream we turn and walk upsteam, that is south-east. We are now on a flat area of ground known as Sand

Parks and here we find the monument previously mentioned, Childe's Tomb. This consists of a roughly shaped granite cross about five feet tall set in a square chamfered socket-stone and standing upon a pile of granite blocks. Some of the blocks have clearly been worked. Beneath these blocks is a chamber which some authorities, including Crossing, believe to be a kistvaen, though not necessarily of prehistoric age. The monument is partly surrounded by a kerb of granite blocks and lying nearby is a fragment—about half—of an ancient and carefully worked socket-stone. Only part of this monument is original, the cross itself for example was made for the purpose when the tomb was restored in the late 19th century. It is doubtful whether, despite its name, anyone was ever buried here. Certain it is that the monument was destroyed early in the 19th century so that the stones might be used in connection with the building of Fox Tor Farmhouse.

Crossing was certain that the stones used to make the bridge by which we crossed the stream came from Childe's Tomb and went to great lengths to trace them. He hoped to persuade people interested to restore the monument by using as much original material as possible but this was not done, much to his justifiable annoyance. He gives the date of the destruction of the original monument as 1812 and says that by the time he came to investigate the matter, in the 1870's, even the site had been forgotten. When he did eventually identify it, only a small mound and some half buried stones were to be seen.

The best known version of the legend of Childe's Tomb has it that the principal character in the drama was one Amyas Childe of Plymstock, who is said to have lived in the reign of Edward III, i.e. in the 14th century. The legend says that Childe was out hunting one day when the party was overtaken by bad weather. Childe became separated from his companions and knowing himself to be lost and in danger of death from exposure, he killed his horse and having disembowelled it, crept inside the carcase for shelter. He froze to death however, but before he died he wrote his will—in blood of course—leaving his estate in Plymstock to whichever church gave his body burial. The legend goes on to say that some men (or perhaps monks) from Tavistock found the body and were conveying it back to Tavistock Abbey for burial when they learned that a plot was afoot to take the body from them so that it might be buried elsewhere. This danger was overcome by a strategem however—the monks threw a bridge across the River Tavy just outside Tavistock where no bridge had been before and the body was safely smuggled into the Abbey and buried there, the estate of Plymstock coming into possession of the monks of Tavistock as a result. This version of the legend was first reduced to writing by Tristram Risdon in his "Survey of the County of Devon", completed about 1630 but not published until 1714.*

In 1946 however Professor H.P.R. Finberg published the results of his own research into the facts behind this legend. Briefly, Professor Finberg discovered that the hero of this drama was probably one Ordulf, son of Ordgar, the Saxon Earl of Devon. (The name Childe is probably derived from Cild—a Saxon title of honour meaning "the young lord".) It seems that it was Ordulf who lost his way and perished in the manner described in the legend. He had already made a will in which he left one of his manors—Antony in Cornwall—to the church where he should be buried and this manor eventually came into the possession of the monks of Tavistock. It is known that Ordulf was alive in 1066 and that the Manor of Plymstock was already in possession of the monks of Tavistock at that time, having been left to them by one Eadwig, brother of King Edmund Ironside, who died during the reign of Canute. From the foregoing it will be seen that the legend of Childe the Hunter is much older than used to be thought and that it is unlikely that the hero was ever buried beneath the monument that bears his name.

According to Risdon, in his day Childe's Tomb bore the following inscription:

"They fyrste that fyndes and bringes mee to my grave,
The priorie of Plimstoke they shall have."

Other authors have quoted somewhat different versions of this inscription but in each case the intent is the same. Writing in the 1820's W. Burt, a well known antiquary of his day, quotes Risdon's version of the couplet but adds that no one then could remember seeing an inscription on the tomb.+ Personally I think it entirely unlikely that Risdon ever visited Childe's Tomb; most likely he was quoting a version of the legend which had been passed on by word of mouth over a period of centuries.

---

* Thomas Westcote also repeats the legend in his *"View of Devonshire"*. This seems to have been completed about 1630 also, but did not reach the printer until 1845.

+ See *Dartmoor, a Descriptive Poem* by N.T. Carrington, with notes by W. Burt. Second edition 1826, published by John Murray, London.

In the churchyard of St. Eustace's Church, Tavistock, is a massive carved arch which always goes by the name of Childe's Tomb or Ordulf's Tomb. This is clearly a remnant of the ancient abbey, the cloisters of which formerly stood upon part of what is now the churchyard. The abbey buildings extended right across what is now the road and took in the site of the present Bedford Hotel. The architecture of the so called Childe's Tomb is said to be of the style attributed to the 13th century, but it seems certain that it was not really a tomb at all but a cloister arch, perhaps the lavatorium or washing place of the monks.

Tavistock Abbey was founded in 981 under royal patronage, but the person most concerned with the foundation was Ordulf, the Saxon ealdorman (or earl) of Devon. This Ordulf's grandson, another Ordulf, lost his life in a snowstorm on Dartmoor, as described above. Both Ordulf the grandfather and Ordulf the grandson have been described as men of great physical strength and Ordulf junior is also said to have been of immense stature. Of Ordulf senior it has been recorded that once, being denied access to the city of Exeter because the city gates had been shut for the night, he broke the bolts to pieces with his bare hands, pulling down part of the wall in the process. He then proceeded to force open the hinges of the gate, shivering the door-posts as he did so.

There is a folk memory, recorded by Mrs. Bray, which tells how, when the foundations of the building that is now the Bedford Hotel were being dug in the early eighteenth century the workmen came across a stone coffin or sarcophagus. This contained, among other bones, two human thigh-bones of great antiquity and unusual length. These were examined as recently as 1914 when they were identified as belonging to two different men. One of the bones had belonged to a man who was of great age at the time of his death; in life he must have been of great strength and stature, standing nearly seven feet in height. The shorter of the two bones also belonged to a very tall man and this may well have been the thigh-bone of Ordulf junior, the Childe of the legend. Who the older man was is of course unknown but he may have been Childe Ordulf's uncle, one Aelfgar the Tall, who was alive in 1066, or some other kinsman.

The stone coffin in which these bones were found may still be seen today, standing under the arch of Betsy Grimbal's Tower, on the opposite side of the road from the church. The coffin is boat-shaped;

it measures only four and a half feet long by 18 inches deep (internal dimensions) and so cannot have been the coffin of either of the giant kinsmen. More likely the bones were collected long after their death and then deposited in the coffin.

In the basement of the arch in the churchyard will be found the sepulchral slab of the Rev. Edward Atkyns Bray, who was Vicar of Tavistock for 45 years. He was the husband of Mrs. Eliza Bray (see footnote)* and was intensely interested in the history and folklore of Tavistock and Dartmoor. It was from his journals that Mrs. Bray extracted much of the information she has passed on to posterity in her book. A more fitting resting place for such a man could hardly have been found.

Leaving Childe's Tomb and perhaps sparing a thought for the young man who lost his way and in consequence his life in this desolate spot nine centuries ago, we now turn away and continue westward, following a path that runs parallel with the wall bordering the newtake on its southern side. As we proceed we have the rising ground topped by Fox Tor on our left and the wide expanse of Fox Tor Mire ahead of us and to our right. This great bog has the reputation of being Dartmoor's most dangerous morass. I can personally vouch for the fact that Fox Tor Mire is very wet and smelly if not treated with proper respect, but I have never known anyone to come to any actual harm here. Animals, cattle and ponies in particular, do fall victim to the bog from time to time however, especially when they are in a weakened condition during a hard winter.

We are in no danger however, as there is a firm path that we can follow along the southern edge of the mire. After about half a mile this brings us to a point where we find our next cross, mounted in a socket cut in a massive boulder. This consists of a short shaft surmounted by a small head, the arms of which expand slightly outward. The head has been broken away from the shaft at some time and is now secured to it by an iron clamp. This cross is now always known as Goldsmith's Cross from the fact that it was re-discovered by Lt. Goldsmith, R.N. in 1903, having been missing for many years. It was found not far from its original position and was

*For the full story of the investigation into the legend of Childe the Hunter see Bray, Eliza, *Traditions of Devonshire* etc. Second edition, 1838, vol. II, p. 113. Also Finberg, H.P.R., *A History of Tavistock Abbey,* 1969, Appendix C, p. 285, and *T.D.A. 78(1946)* p. 265.

set up again in the vacant socket-hole in the boulder.

Goldsmith's Cross stands about 300 yards to the north of the boundary wall of Fox Tor newtake. Beyond the wall, the ground slopes upward to the summit of Crane Hill about a mile to the south. There are numerous great pits and gullies south of the wall, made by the old tin miners and among these will be found a long reave — a bank of earth and stones — which runs east and west. Standing on the line of this reave, at a spot known as Wheal Anne Bottom, is a shaft of granite, nearly six feet tall, upon which has been carved a small cross with equal arms. The top of the pillar, which could very well be the shaft of a typical moorland cross, is uneven, as though part had been broken away. Both Crossing and Masson Phillips record that a shaped stone, probably part of the head of this cross, was found by Dr. Prowse in 1900. This has unfortunately now disappeared. There seems to be no reason for a cross to have been sited at this spot and it seems likely that it once marked the track we are engaged in following and that it was removed to act as a boundary mark for the nearby tin workings. A possible original site for it will be suggested later on.

Returning to Goldsmith's Cross we now continue westward, still following the line of the wall of the newtake. This will bring us, in about a quarter of a mile, to the Devonport Leat, which here flows from north to south. On reaching the stream we turn downstream and soon reach a bridge. We now cross the leat and this brings us into the enclosures of the abandoned Nuns' Cross Farm. We cross the enclosures, having the farmhouse on our left, and soon come to the further side of these when we see, just beyond the ruined perimeter wall the unmistakable shape of Nuns' Cross itself.

As stated earlier, our path divides here. The right-hand arm becomes the Abbots' Way and continues in a north-westerly direction towards Princetown and then on to Tavistock. The left-hand arm follows a course more nearly west, making its way through a complex of tinners works and finally emerges at a spot close to where the Devonport Leat, having flowed through a tunnel about 600 yards in length, comes out into the open again.

Following the leat along with the stream on our left hand, we soon come to a great granite boulder upon which stands the most handsome cross we have seen so far. This is fixed in a socket cut in the boulder. The cross stands about five feet tall; it has a tapering shaft of rectangular section and slightly flattened arms. It is made from a particularly beautiful piece of silver-grey granite. This is clearly not an ancient cross and in fact it bears the inscription "S.L.H. 1887 — 1966". It was set up in 1968 as a memorial to his mother, Mrs. S.L. Hutchinson, by Lt. Commander B. Hutchinson, R.N. with the consent of the interested authorities. This cross has a dual role, for as well as being a memorial, it occupies the original socket of the ancient cross that once stood here, marking the route of the Monks' Path. What happened to the original cross, no-one knows, but is it not possible that the shaft that now stands on the reave in Wheal Anne Bottom, only about a mile away to the east, once occupied this position?

From the cross we have now reached, the true westward line of the old path is somewhat uncertain, for much has happened hereabouts since it was first formed. For one thing the ancient tinners have been hard at work and signs of their activities are everywhere to be seen in the shape of numerous pits, gullies and mounds. Also, the Devonport Leat is a comparatively new intrusion on the scene — it was only constructed in the 1790's. The most likely route for the old path to have taken would seem to be a westerly one, down into the deep valley of the Newlycombe Lake, a stream that rises nearby and flows westward to fall into the Meavy just above Burrator Lake, a couple of miles away. If this route be taken the wayfarer, having crossed the stream in the valley, has to climb the steep side of the valley on the further side to gain the level ground of Walkhampton Common. Here, a few hundred yards beyond the stream will be found our next cross. This stands about six feet tall and is set in a more or less square, rough socket-stone, probably the original. The head and arms and the upper part of the shaft of this cross are original, the lower section of the shaft is a replacement. This cross has no specific name. It stands about 50 yards to the SE of a rough but serviceable track which, running roughly NW — SE across Walkhampton Common, connects the farms and villages in the vicinity of Walkhampton with Princetown and the Forest. No doubt this track was formed, at least in part, along the line of the ancient path we are following. It is still serviceable to-day, even motor vehicles can use it if necessary, owing to the fact that it continued in use long after the monks had gone and was developed by the tinners who were so active in this part of Dartmoor.

Leaving the cross on the common, we make our way to the track just described and turn left along it. After about half a mile, this

Crazywell Cross.

brings us to a spot where, on the high ground to the right of the track and a short distance from it, we see another cross.

The cross we have now reached seems to have no specific name but in recent years it has become known as Crazywell Cross (sometimes Classenwell, sometimes Classiwell), because it stands not far to the east of the famous pool of the same name. Only the head and arms of Crazywell Cross are original, the head is mounted upon a shortish shaft which is a replacement. The arms of the cross expand outward. The cross is set in a rough socket-stone, probably not the original.

We cannot leave this vicinity without a brief visit to Crazywell Pool about which more improbable but romantic legends exist than almost any other place on Dartmoor. Among these is the assertion that the level of the water in the pool rises and falls with the tide at Plymouth and that the pool is bottomless. In the Middle Ages it is said, the pool was the haunt of the Witch of Sheepstor who seems to have given her clients a lot of bad advice. Among them says the legend, was Piers Gaveston, a favourite of Edward II. On the strength of the witch's prognostications, Gaveston, who was rusticating in Devon, rejoined the Court at Warwick where he speedily lost his head to the executioner. The head was set up on the battlements of the castle, thus fulfilling the prophesy that his "humbled head shall soon be high". In fact it seems the pool was probably a tinners' reservoir, most likely of 16th century date or later.

To the west and south-west of Crazywell Pool there stand today many hundreds of acres of conifer plantations. These occupy what were formerly the farmlands of several ancient farms, Stanlake, Roundy, Kingsett and Crazywell among them. The exact route taken by the Monks' Path in this part of Dartmoor is uncertain. It seems likely however that it followed the line of the exisiting track for some distance then veered away to the right and crossed the River Meavy (Crossing calls it the Mew) at a ford near Riddypit where there was probably a farm and certainly a tinners' blowing-house. To-day, although there is a path through the plantations, the river is not readily passable at Riddypit Ford and it is better it take the longer route. This involves following the track westward from near Crazywell Cross, going through the moor-gate and continuing along the side of the plantations for a few hundred yards until a "T" junction is reached. Here we turn right and soon find ourselves approaching the Meavy at a spot where it is spanned by a clapper bridge called Lether Tor Bridge. This bridge is fitted with parapet walls made from slabs of moor-stone (granite) and although not regarded as being particularly ancient it is certainly one of the most picturesque bridges on the Moor. Indeed, the place as a whole is delightful, the combination of ancient trees, grey stone bridge and rushing water presenting a scene of outstanding beauty.

Crossing the bridge, we follow the lane along, in a south-westerly direction. For the first quarter of a mile or so the lane runs through woods, but then the trees on our right fall back and we begin to catch glimpses from time to time of the towering bulk of Lether Tor not far away to the north. At a point about 300 yards from the bridge we see on our right the ruined buildings of Lether Tor Farm and just beyond these, in the bank on the right of the track, we find a small cave. This is nowadays thought to be a potato cave constructed by the farmer at Lether Tor as a frost-free store for his root crops.

About a quarter of a mile beyond the ruins of Lether Tor Farm the track comes into the open and runs parallel with the Devonport Leat which it crossed not far back. Now we reach an intersection where a metalled road coming towards us from the west veers away to the SE and runs steeply downhill to join the road which runs around Burrator Lake.

On the left of the track, near the intersection and on the edge of the plantations we find our next cross. This is the badly mutilated head of an ancient cross fixed upon a tall slim octagonal shaft which is fitted into a massive square socket-stone. The shaft, which appears to be comparatively modern, clearly does not belong to the head or the socket stone. Crossing does not mention this cross and it must be assumed that it was not present in his day. The date of its restoration is unknown. It has no accepted name but the place at which it stands has always been known as Cross Gate. No doubt there was a gate across the road here, giving access to Vennylake Farm, the ruins of which can be found among the trees lower down. It has recently come to light that a cross named Leathertor Cross is mentioned in a parochial return for the parish of Walkhampton dated about 1750. It could be that the cross referred to was the one just described.

Our track now continues westward along the metalled road. About half a mile from Cross Gate we see on our left some ruined

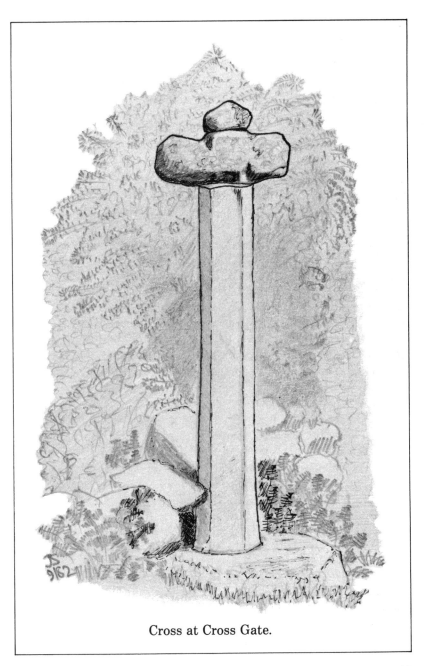

Cross at Cross Gate.

buildings, all that is left of Lowery Farm. There seems to be no doubt that formerly a cross stood opposite the farm. Crossing does not mention it, but Masson Phillips, in his paper of 1937, says that all that was then left of it was a massive granite block which might have served as a pedestal for the cross and a broken stone that might have been part of the socket-stone. In a later paper he reported that the broken socket-stone had now been removed to the foreshore of Burrator Lake, nearby. It has now disappeared.

Before leaving the site of Lowery Farm it might be as well to mention briefly the several abandoned farms referred to above. Most of these, and several others nearby, ceased to operate as agricultural holdings soon after the reservoir (Burrator Lake) was constructed at the end of the 19th century, presumably because of the danger of pollution.

Half a mile west of Lowery the lane reaches a "T" junction where another road comes up from Burrator Lake, making for the Princetown road. Confusingly, the road junction here is named Lowery Cross. We turn right and soon reach another cross roads where our lane meets the B.3212 from Yelverton to Princetown. The name of this junction is Yennadon Cross, from the expanse of open common which lies to the south, called Yennadon Down. On our right as we approach the cross-roads we see another cross. This too is badly mutilated, having lost one arm. It has clearly been used as a gatepost at some time and the holes that once accommodated the gate-hangers are plain to see.

Crossing refers to this cross. He saw it prior to the publication of his book in 1902. It was then built into a wall on Burham Farm, nearby. In 1974 the cross was removed from the wall and re-erected at its present site at the instance of Mr Masson Phillips. This cross stands just under four feet high. It has hollow-chamfered edges and a small cross is incised upon the face. A socket-stone which may be the original belonging to this cross stands near the entrance to Burham Farm on the right of the road a quarter of a mile SW of Yennadon Cross.

While there can be no certainty about it, there is a distinct possibility that the cross just described is in fact the *Yanedone Cross* mentioned in the foundation deed of Buckland Abbey, dated 1280. This was referred to earlier when Marchants' Cross and Nuns' Cross were being discussed.

From Yennadon Cross, Buckland Abbey is almost exactly four

miles distant as the crow flies. A glance at the map will show that the most likely route for the old track to have taken would have been along the line of the present B.3212 road as far as Yelverton (which was not there in those days). The track then probably went by way of Crapstone, bypassing the village of Buckland Monachorum. This part of the route is not marked by any surviving crosses that I am aware of, but there is one more that should be mentioned before we finally leave this part of the Moor.

Running NW from the cross-roads called Yennadon Cross is a lane which if followed will bring the explorer, by a devious route which takes him through a farmyard, to Walkhampton Church. This is a very interesting and typically Dartmoor church situated nearly half a mile north of the village. Adjacent to the church is the old Church House and on the further side of the lane, opposite this, lie the remains of a cross. They consist of the octagonal shaft, which has a square end, and a triangular socket-stone which is completely perforated by the hole intended to take the shaft. Crossing referred to the stocket-stone as being built into a wall near the house in 1902, the shaft came to light later. Both elements were removed from their situation in 1976 and now await restoration and/or re-erection. It is possible that the cross, of which these are fragments, was a wayside cross, perhaps marking a branch of the Monks' Path which, passing near the church, descended into the valley of the River Walkham nearby. The river could be crossed at Huckworthy Bridge and a direct route would then take the traveller to Sampford Spiney or Whitchurch or Tavistock. On the other hand, the cross may have been the ancient churchyard cross belonging to Walkhampton Church. Possibly the desired restoration will have been achieved before this book is published.

In this chapter and the previous one, references have been made to the Foundation Charter of Buckland Abbey and the several crosses mentioned there-in as marking the boundaries of the abbey lands. To clarify the situation and avoid confusion it might be as well to précis what little is known about them. Before doing so however it should be made clear that is is unlikely that all the crosses were erected as boundary markers. It is more likely that most of them were originally way-marks and were adopted as boundary stones at a later date. The crosses referred to in the charter are as follows:-

1. *Crucem Siwardi* — Siwards' Cross — now always called Nuns' Cross. Fully described above.

2. *Smalacumbacrosse* — Smallacombe Cross. This may be the cross now known as Marchants' Cross, which is fully described above. On the other hand one of Dartmoor's foremost authorities, the late Richard Hansford Worth, has stated that he did not think this was so. He advanced the suggestion that *Smalacumbacrosse* might be identical with the present Village cross at Sheepstor. This will be described in a later chapter.

3. *Yanedonecross* — Yannadon Cross. May be identical with the broken cross that now stands at the Yennadon Cross crossroads, described above. Perhaps not at its original site but probably nor far off.

4. *Maynstoncrossa* — Mainstone Cross. This cross is missing and its original site is uncertain. Crossing thought it likely that it was situated somewhere in the vicinity of Bickleigh Vale where there is a wood called Mainstone Wood.

5. *Crucem de Wolewille* — Woolwell Cross. This cross too is missing. Crossing was unable to find any trace of it but both he and Masson Phillips thought that it stood somewhere near Woolwell Farm, which lies about a mile SW of the village of Bickleigh.

6. *Copriscrosse* — Copris Cross. It is thought that this cross occupied a situation about a mile NW of Bickleigh, on Roborough Down near the Tavistock Road. Both Crossing and Masson Phillips describe a socket stone which may have belonged to this cross. This is to be seen in the hedge at the intersection of Leigh Lane and the Bickleigh — Roborough road one mile west of Bickleigh. It is a square socket-stone standing on edge in the hedge-bank and showing a square socket hole. Masson Phillips points out that the position of this stone corresponds more or less with that shown on a 16th century map as being occupied by a cross called *Brokencrosse*. He tentatively suggests that the 16th century *Brokencrosse* may have replaced the 13th century *Copriscrosse*. Nothing is known about the whereabouts of the actual cross.

Chapter 4

Tracks associated with Plympton Priory

Having traced the tracks which linked the monasteries at Buckfast, Buckland and Tavistock, we now turn our attention to the fourth of the religious houses on the immediate perimeter of Dartmoor — Plympton Priory. This Augustinian house was founded in 1121 on the site of a much older collegiate church. At the time of its suppression in 1539 it was the second wealthiest monastery in Devon, Tavistock being the first. Among other possessions the monks of Plympton owned not only the whole of the land upon which the town of Plymouth stood — the town owed its existence to the monks — but also the manors and churches of Meavy, Shaugh Prior and Sampford Spiney. These and four other churches were at first dependent chapels but later became parish churches in their own right. From the foregoing it will be apparent that the monks of Plympton had good reasons for frequent journeyings northward along the western edge of the Moor. Quite apart from business or social visits to their brethren at Buckland and Tavistock, it would have been a matter of plain duty for frequent visits to be paid to Shaugh, Meavy and Sampford Spiney. This would have been a weekly event at least, especially before resident parish priests were appointed. The track that the monks must have used on these occasions still exists, but for by far the greater part of the distance the track is now overlaid by roads. Here and there however the remains of some of the crosses that marked the track can still be found, some of them whole, some mutilated and some probably not at their original positions.

Leaving the village of Plympton St. Mary, which is now virtually a suburb of Plymouth, the track first runs in a north-easterly direction along the line of the Torry Brook. Close to the bridge over the brook near the station the first cross, or all that remains of it, will be found. This consists of an octagonal shaft about five feet high fixed into a rectangular socket-stone which has a chamfered upper edge. There is no trace of the head. The cross shaft and socket are built into the bank of the stream and are often partly embedded in the mud. In view of the proximity of this cross to the bridge it is

49

reasonable to deduce that it marks the site of a former crossing place, probably a ford before the bridge was built.

We leave the crossing place on the Torry and take the road that runs northward out of the village. Half a mile on our journey we pass the entrance to Borringdon on our left and continue northward for about a mile and a half. We then reach a fork in the road and take the left hand branch. This brings us, after another mile, to a road junction called Browney Cross. That a wayside cross once stood here to mark the track is apparent, indeed the socket stone still remains to prove the point. This is octagonal in shape and is nearly four feet across. It is accompanied by three worked stones which probably formed part of the pedestal upon which the cross was mounted. The cross itself is missing. When Crossing wrote in 1902 the stones were in a tumbled neglected condition and this was also the case when Masson Phillips published his first paper in 1937. In 1958 the site was cleared by the County Roads Department and again in 1973. A tablet has now been set up giving information about the cross by the Plympton and District Civic Society.

Half a mile ESE of Browney Cross is a farm called Truelove. This is approached by a long gated lane. On the right hand side of this lane, some distance beyond the gate is the head of a cross, set into the bank. This fragment is two feet two inches tall and about twenty-one inches across the arms. Information is that it was found nearby 50 years ago, having apparently fallen out of the hedge. Nevertheless, it could possibly be that this is the head of the missing Browney Cross.

From Browney Cross the road continues northward for nearly a mile and a half and comes eventually to a cross-roads called Beatland Corner. That another cross stood here at one time is evident from the fact that the socket-stone still remains, on the bank by the roadside. This has a large rectangular socket hole, the edges of which have been broken away. Nothing is known of the whereabouts of the missing cross.

From Beatland Corner, the direct road to Meavy and Sampford Spiney continues northward, but a road also goes off to the NW which passes through the outskirts of Shaugh Prior village and then comes round in a loop to rejoin the road to Meavy. If we take the Shaugh Prior road we shall reach the village in about half a mile. Here, near the vicarage and close to the road junction we shall find another cross. This is about five feet six inches tall and two feet across the arms. The shaft is set in a massive granite socket-stone. Both cross and socket are partly embedded in the wall. This cross clearly has some connection with the parish church which is a short distance to the west, but whether the cross marked the route to the church or perhaps provided a preaching station prior to its building none can say. It may not even occupy its original position.

We now return to the Meavy road, which we do by following the lane that runs NE from the cross. At the first intersection we turn left and very soon find the next cross on our route. This stands on the wide roadside verge to the left (west) of the road, a couple of hundred yards north of the junction. It consists of the upper portion of a cross — head and arms and part of the shaft — set up rather awkwardly upon a replacement shaft which gives it a somewhat gawky appearance. The original part of this cross is three feet long and twenty two inches across the arms. Crossing relates that it was formerly in use as the bottom stone of a stile which stood nearby. He toyed with the idea that this might have been the original cross from Beatland Corner which is about three quarters of a mile away. So it might — the cross and the socket are about right for each other —but this is mere conjecture. The place where it now stands is known as Shaden Moor.

A mile to the north of Shaden Moor the road meets another coming up from the SE, near Cadover Bridge. Originally the road from Cornwood, this has recently been diverted by way of Wotter and Beatland Corner because of china clay working in the area. However, the road is still open to traffic for some distance SE of the bridge and if time permits, a short diversion along it will be rewarded. Standing on the left (east) of the road about two miles SE of Cadover Bridge will be found Blackaton Cross. This consists of a modern shaft, standing in an ancient circular socket-stone and surmounted by the ancient head and arms. The cross stands nearly six feet tall and is about two feet across the arms. It was formerly sometimes known as Roman's Cross but its true name seems to be Blackaton Cross, which Crossing says, comes from a spot nearby called Blackaton Slaggets where much peat was cut in the past. He also relates that there was a tradition in the neighbourhood that St. Paul preached here and adds that he would believe this when it was proved to him that the Saint ever visited Britain.

A further two miles to the SE of Blackaton Cross the road (now closed to through traffic) brings us to a lane on the left leading to

Cross on Shaden Moor.

Cholwich Town Farm. Opposite the entrance to the lane, just clear of the roadside verge, there used to stand a mutilated cross which was formerly in use as a gatepost. This was removed to the spot described in 1969 in the interests of preservation, to join another cross which had also been used as a gatepost. The last mentioned cross had obviously never been completed, having been damaged in the making. The first cross was stolen by some person unknown in 1978 and is still missing. The other is still there. Another mutilated and only partly completed cross is in service as a gatepost at Hanger Farm near Cornwood. The exact purpose of Blackaton Cross and the three crosses mentioned in this paragraph is not clear to me. It may be however, that they served to mark the moorland track connecting Cornwood and other villages in the vicinity with Tavistock and the western side of the Moor.

We now return to Cadover Bridge where our road crosses the Plym en route for Meavy. Immediately north of the bridge and west of the road is a wide expanse of open moorland known as Wigford Down. It seems not unlikely that wayfarers using our track and making direct for Tavistock or perhaps Buckland Abbey might diverge at this point and make their way across Wigford Down in a north-westerly direction. Be that as it may, standing on the down and not far from the road will be found a tall and stately if somewhat damaged cross. The upper two and a half feet of this cross, including the head and arms, is original. The bottom of the shaft is a replacement and is set in the ancient massive circular socket-stone. The cross measures two feet five inches across the arms. The head is damaged in that a section has been split off. At least three small crosses are incised upon the face of this cross. Crossing relates that the upper portion of the cross was found lying on the common by soldiers who were on manoeuvres in 1873 and was set up by them. He says that when he saw the cross in 1901 it had been thrown down by cattle. Its new shaft has clearly been provided since then.

If a north-easterly course be taken across Wigford Down from the cross near Cadover Bridge a mile or so will bring the traveller to a road which, having come up from the Plym Valley, runs NW and eventually arrives at Tavistock via Yelverton and Horrabridge. Close to the spot at which we strike the road is an immense tinners' gulley called Greenwell Gert and nearby, standing on the grassy bank by the roadside will be found the base of another cross. This consists of a massive granite socket-stone, roughly octagonal in shape at the top but rectangular below. Nothing is known about the cross that once stood in this socket. It is in much the same place as it was when Crossing noted it except that it has been moved to a slightly safer position.

Less than a mile to the SW of Greenwell Gert is a farm called Urgles. Here, opposite the farm, will be found a tall modern cross. This stands on the site of an ancient socket-stone which in Crossing's day occupied this position. No doubt the original cross, of which nothing is known, marked a track, now a road, which connected Shaugh Prior with Buckland Abbey by way of a river crossing where Goodameavy Bridge now stands. It seems that the present cross was erected during the present century, perhaps to compensate for the removal of the ancient socket-stone which now stands in the grounds of Goodameavy House acting as the base of a memorial cross to the memory of the son of a previous occupier. It should be noted that Urgles can also be reached, on foot, by taking a westerly route across Wigford Down from Cadover Bridge.

We must now return to the Plympton track which we left at Cadover Bridge to visit Greenwell Gert and Urgles. From the bridge, the track follows the line of the road north and NW across Lynch Common until after two miles of so Marchants' Cross is reached. This has been fully discussed in connection with the Abbots' Way. It marks both tracks.

It seems pretty certain that both the Abbots' Way and the Plympton track passed through Meavy, gaining the village via Marchants' Bridge. This river crossing is picturesque in the extreme. As well as the ancient and beautiful hump-backed packhorse bridge there is a ford and also stepping stones, and a great oak tree overshadows all. In my opinion this is one of the most beautiful spots in the Dartmoor borderland. Beyond the village it seems that the Plympton track continued NW, passing through the village of Walkhampton and crossing the River Walkham at Huckworthy Bridge, another lovely spot. On the high ground a quarter of a mile north of the bridge is a cross roads. Here, travellers bound for Tavistock would go straight on, to join the Abbots' Way on Whitchurch Down. If Sampford Spiney was the destination (it will be remembered that it and Meavy were both part of the possessions of Plympton Priory) the wayfarer would turn right across the common just before the cross-roads was reached. This

Cross on Huckworthy Common.

path follows the line of the hedge on the left and soon brings us to another road junction on Huckworthy Common, where stands the next cross. This is a tall rude cross with very short arms, one of which has been almost completely broken off. It has a small incised cross on one face. The cross stands on a mound of turf close to the road.

The road to Sampford Spiney runs NE from the cross and reaches the church in about a mile. This venerable building is a typical 14th century Dartmoor church, plain and grey and beautiful in its simplicity. There is no village of Sampford Spiney, just a collection of farms and houses scattered over the largely moorland area of the parish. Near the church is the building that was formerly the school, now a dwelling, and the ancient Manor House. On the green, between the church and the school and the Manor House stands a stately granite cross, which Crossing says formerly stood in a hedge nearby. It stands seven feet in height and the arms measure only about twenty inches across. The cross is carefully worked, the shaft being square at the base and octagonal above. Whether this cross was originally the village cross, or a wayside cross one cannot say. Crossing thought that it was probably of 16th century type, and this may be so. But if this is the case, it can hardly have been set up as a preaching station before the church was built. Whatever its function it was clearly regarded as important and to-day it is an additional adornment of a lovely spot. Here the Plympton track ends but the Abbots' Way, en route for Tavistock runs nearby and is connected to it by a lane.

Buckfast to Plympton

Whilst on the subject of ecclesiastical tracks there is yet another of these ancient routes on southern Dartmoor that ought to be mentioned. This one served to link Buckfast Abbey with Plympton Priory. For the first three miles or so this track which as far as I know was never given a name, followed the same line as the Abbots' Way. Having forded the Dean Burn below Cross Furzes however, the track veered away to the left. There is a modern signpost at this spot even now indicating that the left-hand track if followed will bring the traveller to Moor Cross, en route for South Brent. At Moor Cross the track comes out into a border lane and here there is an ancient guide stone with the letters A.P.T. & T cut upon it — indicating the routes to Ashburton, Plympton, Totnes and

Tavistock. For a couple of miles westward of Moor Cross, the old track is lost among lanes. But having crossed the Avon at Shipley Bridge it is next seen at Diamond Lane, a steep, rocky, ramp-cum-stairway which leaves the road a few hundred yards south of Shipley Bridge. This section of the track is about a quarter of a mile long, it then delivers the traveller upon the moor on the eastern slopes of Hickley Ridge. From here the track runs SW, past Coringdon Ball Gate and, skirting the enclosures which lie to the south, it brings the traveller to a ford on the East Glaze Brook and then to another on the West Glaze. From here the exact line of the old track is lost for about a mile, but it must have pursued a roughly south-westerly course before reaching the next point at which it can be identified. Here the traveller coming from the east reaches a well marked track running more or less north and south, which having come up from the southern border hamlet of Wrangaton, extends to the area around Erme Plains and the headwaters of the Erme. Also at or about this point the track we have followed and the one last mentioned are joined by yet another. It too, comes from the east, from Owley Moor Gate in fact, and makes for Harford Moor Gate, as we are.

Standing in a prominent position, as though to mark the junction of the tracks, stands a tall and very unusual cross. Its name is Spurrell's Cross but unfortunately it is far from complete. Indeed, only the head is original and that has lost the whole of one arm and part of the other. The shaft is a modern replacement. But even so there is enough left of the old cross to make quite clear its unusual nature. The head of the cross has a very rough appearance as it is formed from a very coarse grained granite; also the limbs have been so carved as to leave spurs protruding from them. These spurs are about an inch and a half long and two and a half inches wide. This feature makes Spurrell's Cross unique among Dartmoor crosses but there is another with similar spurs or cusps at Ermington Church.

Crossing says that in his day the head of the cross had been set up on a heap of boulders near where it now stands. By the time Masson Phillips described it in 1937 it had been provided with a new shaft by the Dartmoor Preservation Association and was standing where we now see it.

The name of this cross provides another mystery; Crossing tells us that it was sometimes known as Purl's Cross and Baring Gould in his *"Book of Dartmoor"* says that Pearl's Cross was sometimes used. But there seems to be no doubt that its proper name is Spurrell's. As to who Spurrell was or when he lived, all is silence, there being no clue to this in any book that I have ever read. Is the name perhaps a reference to the spurs which adorn the limbs?

From Spurrell's Cross, the track connecting Buckfast with Plympton continues westward. It leaves the Moor at Harford Moor Gate and crosses the Erme at Harford Bridge near Harford Church. Then, skirting the Moor to the north and Hanger Down to the south, it goes by lanes through Cornwood to arrive at Plympton St. Mary by way of Sparkwell and Hemerdon.

It will have been noticed that only one cross now stands to mark the track just described. There is another, however, which was almost certainly associated with it. This is to be found in the churchyard at Harford, standing just inside the gate. It is formed of granite and stands about five feet six inches tall. It is very crudely shaped and both arms are very short, so much so that Masson Phillips describes the cross as having both arms broken off short. Personally, I am not sure about this. I am inclined to think that whoever shaped this cross was content to achieve the rough appearance of a cross without going to too much trouble over it — as with Bennet's Cross and a number of others. The cross at Harford was found several years ago, doing duty as a gatepost in the lane leading from the church to the moor-gate, though the cross itself bears no signs of this use. I used to think it probable that the original situation of this cross was on the Moor marking the track we have just followed. But having recently re-examined the spot from which, according to local information, the cross was removed, I am not now so sure about the matter.

The gateway in question is on the right-hand side of the lane as one proceeds from the church to the moor-gate. Inside the gate are the remains of a hedge-bank and other signs which indicate that in former days a stroll between the enclosures would have followed the now existing hedges and brought the stroll out onto the open moor a couple of hundred yards to the south of the present moor-gate. If the proposition be accepted that this stroll was the route by which the ancient track came to join the lane near the church, then the junction of the stroll with the lane would be the natural place for a waymark to be sited. That this was a frequent practice has been illustrated in this and previous chapters.

Crossing does not mention the Harford Cross; but he describes

Harford Church in his book about crosses and this can only mean that he was unaware of its existence. An elderly resident told me quite recently, that although she could not be specific as to dates, she thought its finding and removal took place about fifty years ago.

Whilst we may have some doubt about how much or how little the old monks used the track between Buckfast and Plympton there is another aspect of it which must be of interest. In his paper on *Dartmoor Tracks and Guide Stones* Richard Hansford Worth comments that the Train-bands, the 17th and 18th century version of the Militia, on their way from Exeter to Plymouth, passed through Ashburton and Buckfastleigh, then by Yalland Farm to Shipley, crossed the Avon and proceeded by way of Diamond Lane . . . to the ford at Glasscombe Corner; thence by Spurrell's Cross to Harford Moor Gate, where they returned to the enclosed lands. In other words they used a large portion of the route just described and our ancient track served the country in its hour of need.

Since this chapter was originally prepared we learn that Blackaton Cross (see page 51) is likely to be moved to a different site nearby. It is in danger of being engulfed by china clay waste from adjacent works.

Beetor Cross.

Chapter 5

Other tracks marked by crosses—the road from Exeter to Tavistock

Having dealt with the crosses along the four important tracks that can be identified as having served as links between the religious houses on the borders of Dartmoor — the Abbots' Way, the Monks' Path, the Plympton Track and the Buckfast—Plympton track, we now turn to tracks and crosses in a somewhat different category.

Standing along lanes and roads around the perimeter of the Moor, and especially in the eastern and north-eastern quadrant, are many old crosses about whose ancient history practically nothing is known. Allowing for the inevitable gaps arising from the removal and/or destruction of some crosses over the centuries, nevertheless sufficient still remain to enable us to trace several routes marked by the crosses. Some of these are ancient through-routes; for example, the track across the Moor, now the B.3212 road, linking Exeter with Chagford and Moretonhampstead and then on to Tavistock and beyond. The modern road was engineered largely along the line of the ancient track except that Chagford was ignored and left isolated by the turnpike road which came through Moretonhampstead.

Today, three ancient crosses stand by or close to the B.3212. The whereabouts of the remains of a fourth are known and there is a record of a fifth, now missing.

The sites of all five crosses referred to above were along the section of road between the village of Postbridge and a cross-roads known as the Watching Place, (where the B.3344 from Bovey Tracey joins the B.3212) a distance of about five miles. The B.3344 is always known locally as Long Lane, a very apt name. As well as serving Bovey Tracey, this road also helps to connect Chagford with Ashburton and this was originally probably its most important role.

Both Chagford and Ashburton were Stannary Towns and deeply involved in the locally important tin trade. Both towns had woollen mills and around Ashburton were important lime kilns whose product was much needed on the thin acid soils on the borders of Eastern Dartmoor. Consequently it is not surprising that the cross-roads just referred to, which bears the evocative name of The Watching Place, should have been chosen as the site for a wayside cross. The cross is still there, having been removed at some time and erected in a nearby field to do duty as a gatepost. It was restored to what was presumed to be its original position in 1899. This is a very rude cross indeed; it has very short unequal arms, one of which is higher than the other. The shaft is short, not more than five feet I should say, and part of the head and part of one arm are missing. The cross stands high on the roadside bank at the SE corner of the junction. Its name is Beetor Cross.

According to Crossing, there was in his day a local tradition that the cross was erected to commemorate a battle between the native British and the invading Saxons. This would make the cross very ancient indeed, perhaps as early as 7th century, which is unlikely. More likely it marked the intersection of two important tracks. There is also a tradition that the name of the junction is a survival from the days when a gallows stood at this spot where sorrowing relatives waited until they were allowed to remove the body of the person who had been executed. Another story is that a rider on horseback who passes this spot is likely to find that his horse rears in alarm when a ghostly hand grasps the bridle. Motorists are immune it seems.

The Watching Place is not truly a cross-roads but a "T" junction. A few yards to the north another road goes off to the NW, towards Chagford. Just to confuse the explorer the "T" junction so formed is called Beetor Cross, which it will be remembered is also the name of the cross just discussed.

We now make our way SW along the B.3212 towards Postbridge. About a mile from The Watching Place we see, on the left, a house by the roadside ahead of us. Alongside the house is a gated lane and mounted on the bank by the gate is a cross. This is Leeper Cross, so called because it was found built into a wall at Leeper Farm (now called Moorgate) to which the lane and the track beyond lead. Crossing records that when he wrote, this cross was built into the wall at the farm. In his paper of 1937, Masson Phillips continues the story. It seems that in the early years of the present century the cross was removed from Leeper (I learn that this was done at the instance of the then Lord of the Manor, Viscount Hambledon) to the Manor House at North Bovey. In 1937, the Manor and Manor House having changed ownership, the cross was returned to Leeper and was subsequently set up near the road, where we see it to-day. The cross is only about four feet tall and is twenty two inches across the arms. It is roughly constructed of granite and one arm is broken short. There is a raised cross on each face. Whether it now stands at its original place is unknown but it may well be so. Interestingly enough, the place at which Leeper Cross now stands is the spot where the Exeter/Tavistock road is crossed by the medieval track known as the Mariners' Way, which is said to have connected the ports on the north coast of Devon with those on the south coast. This might have been an additional reason for siting a cross here.

From Moorgate the road continues SW and begins to rise, reaching its highest point near Warren House Inn, a little over two miles away. The road runs over open moorland until it reaches the out skirts of Postbridge, passing as it does so two road junctions, one on the left and one on the right. These "T" junctions are named Challacombe Cross and Chagford Cross respectively but neither is the site of a cross to-day, nor am I aware of any suggestion that crosses were ever sited at either. The roads lead to the places from which the junctions take their name, a commonplace fact in this part of the world. At Chagford Cross is an ancient and interesting guide stone that is worth examination.

From Chagford Cross, the road continues its undulating course with high ground to the right (north) and mainly falling ground to the left. Soon the road begins to run almost dead straight and at the end of the straight stretch we see the Warren House inn ahead of us in the near distance, on the right of the road. On the left of the road, about four hundred yards short of the Inn, stands our next cross. This is Bennet's Cross. It stands well back from the road close to a recently constructed roadside car-park. This is a very odd cross, indeed it is one of those mentioned earlier, in which a minimum of work has been done to a pillar of granite to give it a cross-like appearance. This one stands about six feet tall and has a rough, bulky, semi-round semi-rectangular shaft. The shaft has a decided kink in it. The arms are very short and both they and the head taper slightly. The letters WB are carved on the shaft. According to Crossing, they signify "Warren Bounds" and other stones bearing the same initials can be found on the common nearby. The ancient rabbit warren from which Warren House Inn took its name lies to the immediate south.

How Bennet's Cross got its name is uncertain. It might be no

Bennet's Cross.

more than that a local tin-miner named William Bennet held mining rights in the vicinity and that the cross was one of his bound-stones. It is said that a tinner of this name appears in a 16th century Stannary record as having attended a meeting of the Stannary Parliament. On the other hand, the track marked by this and other crosses along the road was the direct connection between Exeter, where there was a Benedictine monastery and Tavistock, where there was another. Bennet (or Benet) was a common corruption of the name Benedict in medieval times, so this explanation too could be acceptable. Again, it is interesting to note that the ancient track coming from Chagford and making for Tavistock, across the open moor, joined the road that we are following near this spot. This again could have a bearing on the question as to why a cross should be sited here. Bennet's Cross is also a boundary mark; it stands on the boundary between the parishes of North Bovey and Chagford.

In Bennet's Cross we have the last remaining cross going westward along the old Exeter/Tavistock track until we reach the Windypost near Pew Tor which we visited when we traversed the Abbots' Way. Formerly however, there were at least two more crosses along this road. One of these stood on Merripit Hill, between Warren House Inn and Postbridge, about a mile from the village. There is more than one record of this cross which is said to have stood on the south side of the road. It was seen by the husband of the author of Mrs. Bray's *Borders of the Tamar and the Tavy* on 27th July 1831. He described it as being nine and three quarters feet in length; it had very short arms but was of more regular shape and better wrought than most such crosses on the moor. It was then fallen and lying near a circular pit.

Crossing tells us how he questioned an elderly resident, Jonas Coaker the Dartmoor Poet, who died in 1890, about this cross. Jonas remembered the cross. He said that it used to stand on Merripit Hill but was removed from there to Postbridge and used as a post for the toll-gate. When the toll-gate was removed, the posts disappeared and Crossing was unable to find out what happened to them. It may be that they were built into some building and the cross may even yet come to light.

Continuing westward, we now come to to the hamlet of Postbridge. Here on the right (north) of the road, not far from the East Dart Hotel, will be found two tiny cottages, always known as the Stannon Lodges. These were built about the turn of the

18th/19th centuries to serve as gate lodges at the entrance to the drive of what was to have been a mansion at Stannon, about three quarters of a mile away. The mansion was never built and a cottage was erected on the site, but the lodges remained. They have recently been rebuilt. Mr Bray says he saw another cross near here and Jonas Coaker told Crossing that he too remembered the cross but did not know what became of it.

This cross was known as Maggie Cross — presumably Margaret's of St. Margaret's Cross. In recent years attention has been drawn to the hedge near the westernmost of the Stannon Lodges and in particular to one stone in the hedge. This is said to be all that remains of Maggie Cross. I can only say that there is something odd about one of the stones but that I find it difficult to positively identify it as part of a cross. As previously stated, there are no more crosses, or records of them, west of Postbridge for several miles.

Although Postbridge qualifies only as a hamlet and not a particularly ancient one at that, it and the road that runs through it are associated with many strange stories. Reference has already been made to the ghostly hand that tugs at the reins of horsemen in the vicinity of The Watching Place. Then there are the Hairy Hands which grip the steering wheels of motor vehicles near Cherry Brook Bridge and force the vehicles off the road. Postbridge itself has a black dog — bloodhound? — which arrives at the village in the small hours of every morning and laps up the liquor spilt in the ditch opposite the East Dart Hotel by the long suffering landlord whose teetotal wife nagged him until he could stand no more. As a result the pub, once the Greyhound Inn and later Webb's Hotel, became a temperance hotel for many years.*

West of Postbridge it seems likely that the medieval Exeter/Tavistock track followed the line taken by the present road, at least as far as Two Bridges. Here there was a ford over the West Dart, and later a bridge, probably a clapper, the forerunner of the arched bridges now to be found there. The origin of the place-name, Two Bridges, has given rise to much conjecture in the past, the question being which two bridges does the name refer to. Today the place-names authorities tend to think that the name is probably a

---

* All these and many other fascinating stories can be found in a little booklet *Tales of a Dartmoor Village* by Theo Brown. They originally formed the thesis of a paper in the *Transactions of the Devonshire Association* for 1961 (Vol.93).

corruption of *Tobrygge,* a version dating back to the reign of Henry VI and meaning simply "at the bridge".

Beyond Two Bridges the track veered away northward and crossed the Cowsic river just below Beardown Farm where today there is a charming little clapper bridge of five openings, restored in the late 19th century after being swept away by a flood. Continuing westward the track took a line about half a mile to the north of the present road and crossed the Blackbrook at a spot where today the prison enclosures lie. Until about two years ago an ancient clapper bridge spanned the brook. This now lies in the stream awaiting restoration when funds and time become available. Close by is a feature well known in Dartmoor lore, Fice's Well (more properly Fitz's Well). Here a granite canopy bearing the date 1568 and the initials I.F. (John Fitz) has been erected over a stone basin filled from a nearby spring. A circular wall has been built around the monument to protect it from the attentions of cattle. The story is told how Sir John Fitz of Fitzford and his wife were led astray by the pixies whilst crossing this part of the Moor. They were rescued from their predicament by drinking the water from the spring, which had magic qualities. Later as an act of gratitude Sir John had the canopy erected over the spring for the benefit of future wayfarers. We shall meet Sir John again when we visit another similar site near Okehampton.

Beyond Fitz's Well the track presumably traversed the southern slopes below Great Mis Tor and came down to the River Walkham at or near the spot where Merrivale Bridge now stands. Westward of Merrivale the track from Exeter almost certainly joined the one from Ashburton and Buckfast — the Abbots' Way — en route for Tavistock.

In 1985, Bennet's Cross (see page 63) was damaged, possibly by lightning. It has been repaired but part of the inscription is now obliterated.

Sanduck Cross.

Chapter 6

Tracks marked by crosses—continued—Lustleigh and North Bovey

We now shift the scene of our investigations and make for the village of Lustleigh. This ancient and beautiful picture-postcard village lies in the valley of the River Wrey about three miles north of Bovey Tracey. In the centre of the village, facing the Church, is the village green and upon the green stands a cross which looks for all the world like a very well preserved village cross. It is not however; it is a memorial to the Rev. Henry Tudor, sometime Rector of Lustleigh, who died early in the present century.

Lustleigh in fact has no village cross, but near a cross-roads just to the north of the village is an ancient stone which at some time may have been the pedestal of a considerable cross. This stone, always known as the Bishop's Stone, is a large block of granite. The upper part has been carefully dressed but the lower part is left rough. It is octagonal above and square below. The upper surface is quite flat; no socket has been cut in it but it could be that the stone formed the platform upon which the socket-stone stood. On one face a coat of arms has been incised. At present this is indecipherable because of the lichen that has formed over it but Crossing thought that it represented the arms of Bishop Grandisson, a 14th century Bishop of Exeter. Masson Phillips says that the arms are apparently those of Bishop Cotton of Exeter (1598—1621). There is no evidence one way or the other but the Bishop's Stone certainly looks like the base of a substantial and important cross.

Leaving the Bishop's Stone, we take the road which runs southward, but instead of entering the village, we turn up a lane on our right which leads us up Mapstone Hill and away from Lustleigh. This is a narrow winding lane and in places very steep. But eventually we find the land levelling out and then at a distance of about a mile and a half from the village we reach a place called Higher Combe where there are a couple of cottages on the right of the road. Just before the cottages are reached there is a field gate on the same side of the road. Looking over the gate we see, standing on a rock in the field, the head and arms and a short piece of the shaft of an ancient cross. It is said that the cross was mounted on the boulder in 1860 and that it formerly stood in the bank of the same field. The field is known as Cross Park. The original site of this cross is unknown but I should think it pretty certain that it formerly marked the track that is now the road along which we came. But where did this track go to, or come from? Let us follow it and see.

Almost exactly a mile northward of Higher Combe the road brings us to a farm called Sanduck, standing at a point where the road makes an almost right-angled turn to the west. Just beyond the farmhouse, on the right of the road under a tree stands the next cross — Sanduck Cross. This is a carefully made cross with chamfered shaft and arms. One arm has been broken off and a replacement fitted. The cross is about five feet tall and stands in what is said to be a modern socket-stone. According to Crossing, Sanduck farmhouse was burned down in 1901 and the cross was found in the foundations, presumably when the site was being cleared prior to re-building, which took place in 1902. We are given no clue as to the age of the farmhouse that was burned, but it was probably 17th century, very many Dartmoor farmhouses having been rebuilt at about that period. There is no evidence as to how the cross came to be in the foundations of the house but one likes to think that perhaps the residents of Sanduck, being aware of the cross-breaking activities of the Puritans, removed the old cross to a place of safety until the arrival of better times. If so, they succeeded in their aims, but were a couple of centuries late in achieving them.

From Sanduck, the road continues westward for about a quarter of a mile and then divides. We take the left hand arm and follow the road — which runs above and parallel with Lustleigh Cleave — for about a mile, when we arrive at a farm entrance on the right. This is the entrance to South Harton Farm; it has massive gate-pillars and an air of consequence. Alongside and to the right of the gateway stands a cross. This is a tall rudimentary specimen standing six feet three inches tall and twenty inches across the arms.

The cross is partly built into the wall against which it stands. It has one very unusual feature in that at some time it has been split down the middle, from top to bottom, probably to form a pair of gateposts. In the 19th century the two halves were carefully re-assembled and the cross erected where we now see it, by a previous occupier of South Harton. It seems unlikely that South Harton Cross now stands at its original position; my own feeling is that it

South Harton Cross.

probably came from somewhere along the lane that we followed from Lustleigh via Higher Combe and Sanduck, where, if my theory is correct, it would serve a useful purpose.

We now retrace our route as far as the fork in the road near Sanduck and then take the lane that runs NW from the junction. We are now bound for the village of North Bovey. This we reach by following the road for a couple of miles until it brings us to a cross-roads where we turn left. The cross-roads, in true Devon fashion, is named Bovey Cross, and at the cross-roads stands a cross — Horsepit Cross. This is a short stumpy specimen with short arms and a truncated head. The cross has been turned into a direction post by having the letters O (Okehampton), N (Newton Abbot), M (Moretonhampstead), and B (Bovey) carved upon the two faces and the ends of the arms of the cross. This was probably an 18th/19th century defacement, the cross is obviously much older than that. As to the name of this cross; William Crossing says that the field at whose gate the cross stands was called Horse Pit and that the name was applied to the cross also. Personally, I don't like this explanation but of course I cannot disprove it. But — was there perhaps a hospice for travellers along one of the lanes radiating from the cross-roads? I don't know but I find this possibility more pleasing than the other.

From Bovey Cross, a little over half a mile brings us into the village of North Bovey. This is another beautiful spot; venerable church, thatched houses, village green with ancient oaks, make the perfect setting for the granite cross that stands upon the green. This occupies a socket-stone that was clearly made for a different type of cross. The socket is carefully worked, it is square below and octagonal above and is intended to take a cross having a rectangular shaft with chamfered corners. This cross has a plain rectangular shaft which only half fills the socket. The socket-stone obviously belonged to the village cross, now missing. It is said, however, that the broken head of the old cross is built into the wall of the parlour of the cottage opposite the cross. The cross that we now see upon the green was found in the early 19th century doing duty as a footbridge across a stream just below the village. It probably originally stood near a ford across the river Bovey, to mark the way. This ford can be reached by taking (on foot) the lane that runs SE out of the village. It is a wonderful, romantic spot where there is one of the best sets of stepping-stones I know. If followed, the track alongside the ford brings the traveller, by way of a farm called Fursdon, to the road along which we came from Sanduck to Bovey Cross.

From the village green at North Bovey, we take the lane that runs southward out of the village. This brings us in a couple of hundred yards or so to a bridge at the foot of the hill. Here the road divides, one branch going over the bridge, the other turning right and running alongside the stream (the River Bovey). We take the latter and follow it to a "T" junction where we turn left and cross the river by a bridge. We now continue along the lane to the hamlet of Yard, passing as we go an old mill on the right of the road with its water-wheel still in position. Yard is a small collection of ancient farms and houses clustered round a green upon which four lanes or tracks converge. We take the road that runs west and in about a quarter of a mile notice a very rough lane upon our left. This leads to two farms, named Higher and Lower Langdon. Until just a few years ago (my diary tells me that I saw it on 14th August, 1968) an ancient and badly mutilated cross stood in the farmyard at Lower Langdon. The cross was doing duty as a gatepost when I saw it. One arm was missing and the cross generally presented a very battered appearance. In 1980 I went to have another look at this cross but it had gone. The farm had changed hands by this time and the new occupier knew nothing about the cross at all. There is no information as to where this cross came from in the first place but I think it entirely unlikely that it originated at Langdon. A much more likely place would have been near Yard, at the intersection of four tracks, marking the one that we have followed from Lustleigh.

We now return to Yard and take the lane that runs NW. After about a third of a mile the road runs into a wood and down into the valley of a stream — a branch of the Bovey. Having crossed the stream the road rises again and having passed Bowden Mill on the left brings us to a cross-roads. Close to the junction and raised upon a high masonry bank to the right of the road stands a cross. This is Hele Cross, which takes its name from Hele Farm a few yards away. This is a very good specimen; it is a Maltese Cross with an octagonal shaft and arms, standing in a socket-stone square at the base and octagonal above. The cross stands five feet ten inches high and measures twenty five inches across the arms.

Crossing tells us that in his day there was a tradition in the neighbourhood that a small chapel once stood near the stream that

Hele Cross.

runs nearby, and that the cross was brought from here. Around the cross, people bound on a pilgrimage to Tavistock Abbey used to gather to offer prayers before setting out across the moor. We are never likely to know whether there is any truth in this old story or not, but it is at least possible. Accepting this, we can also accept that people making for Hele as a gathering place and coming from Lustleigh, North Bovey and so on would probably have taken the route we have followed. From this it is but a step to asking whether perhaps the Bishop's Stone at Lustleigh was itself a mustering place for pilgrims bound for Hele and then on to Tavistock. From Hele the route to Tavistock would lie along the lane which runs due west from Hele.* Half a mile along this lane brings the traveller to the Watching Place and Beetor Cross. Here of course he joins the main track from Exeter to Tavistock, which we traversed earlier on.

---

* The place-name Hele is a common one in Devon. According to the authors of *The Place Names of Devon* it means, in general terms, a corner or angle; a retired or secret place. The Hele we have just visited qualifies, it is indeed an out of the way place.

Cross on Week Down.

Chapter 7

Wayside crosses in the Chagford area

We now take the B.3212 road from The Watching Place and follow it NE for about two miles in the direction of Moretonhampstead. We soon reach a cross-roads named Thorn Cross and here we turn left and follow the lane north and north-west until we reach a farm called Middlecott. Here we turn hard left and note that the road immediately begins to rise. At a point about a quarter of a mile beyond Middlecott we find our first cross, standing by the roadside, close to the verge on the right of the road. This is quite different from any cross we have examined so far, indeed the casual observer would probably not recognise it as a cross at all. It consists of a slab of granite about six feet tall and eighteen inches wide. Indeed, the word monolith has been applied to it. The two long sides of this slab are not straight but slightly curved. On one face is a cross in relief; this is about twenty one inches long and thirteen inches across the arms. In the centre of this cross a small cross with equal arms has been cut. On the opposite face is another incised cross. The cross is known as Short or Shorter Cross.

Short Cross was described by Ormerod in 1874. He tells us that at the time of writing it was in use under a pump at Middlecott Farm, having been removed from its proper place in 1873. Crossing says that in 1873 the cross was removed from under the pump and taken back to its original position. Masson Phillips says that in his opinion, this is one of Devon's earliest crosses, possibly of Saxon origin and of 7th—9th century date.

A little way beyond Short Cross, the road passes through a gateway and we now find that we are traversing a piece of open common which lies to the right of the road. This is Week Down and here we find our next cross. This is on the right of the road and stands on the edge of the common. It consists of a tall rectangular shaft of granite, six feet nine inches tall. It has a rounded head and two very short arms have been cut out of the shaft. A Maltese Cross is cut on each face; one of these is in line with the shaft of the cross which is inclined at an angle to the ground, the other is at right-angles to the ground. This rather strange fact led Ormerod (who described the cross in 1874, having known it from at least 1859) to conjecture that the crosses had been carved after the cross was erected and had settled down to its out of perpendicular stance. Ormerod also tells us that the cross was in danger of falling in 1867 and that it was then moved back from the road a little but that its original angle of inclination was repeated when it was re-erected. He says too, that there was a project afoot to move the cross and use it to make a foot-bridge; happily it was spared this fate. We find the 19th century mentality that led so many people of the period to happily destroy antiquities of this kind for purely utilitarian purposes extraordinary. The fact may serve to remind us however, that vandalism is not a new phenomenon, even on Dartmoor.

The road across Week Down, alongside which Short Cross and the one just described both stand, provided a direct route from both Moretonhampstead and North Bovey to Chagford. This would have been particularly the case at a time when Chagford was an important place and all wayfarers were either on foot or horseback. The crosses therefore, would serve as way-marks along a track used by many people. This track would also have been used as a church path by the dwellers at many of the outlying farms in the district.

Before leaving the vicinity of Chagford, there are a couple of other wayside crosses which should be mentioned. The first of these stands on top of a high bank above and to the left of the road as one approaches Leigh Bridge about a mile west of Chagford. Only the head and arms of this cross are original. The fragment is mounted on a rough replacement shaft of rectangular section. This cross clearly does not now occupy its original position. I am told by Mr John Somers Cocks that the head of the cross was brought from Teigncombe, a mile and a half further west, in the early days of the present century. This was done at the instance of a Mr Clampitt who caused it to be erected where it now stands.

A visit to Teigncombe is now indicated. This ancient hamlet is reached by following the road which runs SW out of Chagford and then continues by way of Thorn and Yeo to Teigncombe. Here, on the left of the road just before the cluster of buildings is reached, will be seen a field gate. Have a close look at the gateposts. One of these is a more or less circular slab of granite which is perforated by a rectangular hole about a foot square. This is almost certainly the base of a wayside cross, similar to several others around Dartmoor, Mr. Somers Cocks tells me that he believes that this base belongs to

Gatepost at Gidleigh.

the cross near Leigh Bridge and that the cross originally stood at Teigncombe. To me this seems entirely likely. A chapel existed nearby in medieval times and the Mariners' Way, the ancient track connecting North and South Devon also passed this way. It would seem to be a natural site for a wayside cross.

Half a mile west of Teigncombe lies the open moor, represented here by Chagford and Gidleigh Commons. The moor-gate can be reached by following Teigncombe Lane which gives access to a part of Dartmoor absolutely packed with objects of interest, both antiquarian and natural. This is not the place for a description of these but a few lines of verse descriptive of the lane itself would not perhaps be out of place. They are culled from Sabine Baring-Gould's *Book of Dartmoor* and go as follows:

> "Tincombe Lane is all up hill
> Or downhill, as you take it;
> You tumble up, and crack your crown,
> Or tumble down and break it.

> Tincombe Lane is crook'd and straight,
> Here pothook, there as arrow,
> 'Tis smooth to foot, 'tis full of rut,
> 'Tis wide and then, 'tis narrow.

> Tincombe Lane is just like life,
> From when you leave your mother;
> 'Tis sometimes this, 'tis sometimes that,
> 'Tis one thing or the other."

To-day Teigncombe Lane is a good tarmac road; it must have been very different in the days when it was the main route off the moor for the carts laden with peat for the farms and villages around. But if the explorer wants to see what a genuine old Dartmoor track was like he can still do so. A few hundred yards to the SE and running parallel with Teigncombe Lane is Featherbed Lane. This starts at the hamlet of Teigncombe and debouches upon Chagford Common after a steep pull-up of about a quarter of a mile. This lane can best be described as a cross between a wide rut and a rocky staircase. Down it used to come the packhorses laden with peat in the days when wheels were practically unknown upon Dartmoor — that is about 200 years ago.

The other cross in the vicinity of Chagford that I want to mention is to be found near the bridge over the Blackaton Brook by the side of the road that leads from Throwleigh to Chagford and about a mile and a quarter SE of the village of Throwleigh. Here, west of the bridge and on the north side of the road will be found the cross we are looking for. It consists of part of the shaft and one arm of a cross of rectangular section. This fragment is twenty nine inches high and nineteen inches across the shaft and the arm that remains. When complete it would have measured about twenty three inches across the arms. Incised upon one face is a cross with arms of equal length enclosed within a circle which is twelve inches in diameter.

The Blackaton cross was found built into the wall upon which it now stands in the 1950's. Apparently the cross came to light when the wall collapsed and had to be re-built. Later, it was erected where we now see it. The original site of this cross is unknown. Ormerod described a somewhat similar fragment in 1874, but Mr. Masson Phillips, having compared the description with the Blackaton cross, cannot reconcile the two and we must therefore accept that they are different.

There are other crosses in this part of the world, in the churchyard at Chagford and in Throwleigh village for example. They will be dealt with in subsequent chapters when churchyard and village crosses are being discussed.

The two crosses at West Wyke.

Chapter 8

Wayside crosses around Northern Dartmoor

For the purposes of this chapter, we first of all make for a farm called West Wyke. This lies to the south of the A.30 (Exeter to Okehampton) road about a mile and half from the village of South Zeal. A narrow lane runs past the farmhouse which is an ancient and beautiful granite building with a battlemented entrance. It was formerly a manor house, the seat of the Battishill family. Close by the entrance to the farm and standing under a tree will be seen two crosses. They are both in a battered condition, indeed, one of them is a mere fragment, but apart from this they are as different as two crosses could be. One of them, the shorter, consists only of the arms, and part of the shaft of a carefully sculptured cross which has been erected so that it stands upright. It is fixed upon a mound of earth faced with stones and measures thirty two inches across the arms. The arms and shaft are octagonal in section and it is obvious that this was originally a cross of some importance. Ormerod described this cross in 1874; it occupied the same position then that it does to-day. Neither he nor Crossing, who also described it, make any reference to its original position and I have never succeeded in finding out anything about it.

The other cross at West Wyke stands quite close to the former. It is a roughly shaped cross of rectangular section. It stands about five feet high and tapers almost to a point at the top. One arm has been broken off and the other is very short indeed. A cross about nineteen inches tall has been incised upon one face in a rather lopsided fashion. On the other face is a somewhat shorter cross. Neither Ormerod nor Crossing make any reference to this cross. Masson Phillips described it as he saw it in 1937 when it was doing duty as a gatepost near where it now stands, and again in 1959. The marks of the gatehangers are still plain to see, as are other marks which seem to indicate that it has served in more than one role. It was removed and re-erected in its present position in 1958. Although the original use and site of this cross are unknown, it is typical of the rude wayside crosses to be found in considerable numbers in the lanes and approach roads around Dartmoor. It is unlikely that it has been moved very far over the centuries.

From West Wyke we cross the A.30 road and take a lane that runs northward to the hamlet of Addiscott. Here, standing at the cross-roads is our next cross. Addiscott cross is a fine specimen. It stands only about four feet eight inches tall but it has been carefully fashioned and is splendidly proportioned. It measures eighteen inches across the arms which are of octagonal section as is the upper part of the shaft. The cross stands in the ancient rectangular socket-stone. This cross has had a somewhat chequered career. In 1874 when Ormerod described it, it had recently been moved from a position nearby and re-erected, apparently to save it from a worse fate. Crossing saw it as Ormerod did and when Masson Phillips wrote in 1937 it was still in the same position. Later in 1958, it was moved to its present position which is certainly more satisfactory than the last. It seems likely that Addiscott cross and others in the vicinity, now to be described, marked the Church Path to South Tawton from the farms and hamlets in the valley of the River Yeo or perhaps even for travellers from further afield.

From Addiscott Cross, we take the lane that runs northward and follow it for nearly a mile. This brings us to a cross-roads close to the ancient manor house of the Oxenham family, now a farm. This place is famous as being the scene of the appearance of the White Bird of the Oxenhams, which is said to appear at or near the bedside of a member of the family who is at death's door. At the cross-roads we turn right and continue eastward for rather less than half a mile. Here, on the left of the road at a "T" junction stands another wayside cross. This is a much plainer specimen than the last. It has no proper name but it is always known as the cross at Ringhole Copse. It is tall, nearly seven and half feet in height and it measures nineteen inches across the arms. The arms are short in proportion to the shaft which is rectangular in section.

Ormerod thought that this cross was probably in its original position and I agree with him. The remarks about the purpose of Addiscott Cross apply here also.

In 1982, whilst a friend and I were checking the crosses in this vicinity she (the friend) noticed that at a point about a quarter of a mile west of Ringhole Copse a footpath coming from the north-east joins the road. On investigation it became apparent that the footpath follows the line of an ancient lane or stroll, obviously long disused. This lane had clearly once been gated and close to the road but partly hidden by the high hedge was one of the gateposts. This is roughly but definitely octagonal in shape and tapers upwards. The top of the post is rough as though it had been broken off so as to leave a blunt point. I think there is little doubt that in this post we see all that remains of yet another wayside cross, placed as is so often the case at a point where the track it marks joins another track or road.

We now turn westward and follow the lane back, past Oxenham to another cross-roads about three hundred yards beyond the Addiscott turning. Here is yet another cross, set up on a high bank to the left of the road at the cross-roads. This is Oxenham Cross; it consists of the shaft and head of a small rough cross of octagonal section. The cross has clearly been broken across the shaft and repaired. In Ormerod's day only the portion of the shaft was to be seen. Crossing describes how he found the upper part of the cross among some stones in a hedge nearby. This was some years prior to the publication of his book in 1902. Masson Phillips, writing in 1937 tells us that the two sections of the cross had by that time been cemented together and lay upon the top of the hedge. Later, in 1954, he describes how the cross was restored (it was now broken again) and re-erected in its present position at the instance of the Dartmoor Preservation Association. This took place in 1951 and Mr Masson Phillips himself supervised the restoration. I think it is a reasonable assumption that Oxenham Cross to-day stands somewhere near its original site. South Tawton church is only about three quarters of a mile distant, due west.

Just to the west of Oxenham Cross lies the village of South Tawton, which we shall visit in a later chapter, and half a mile south of that, its daughter village South Zeal. A lane connects the two villages and at a fork about mid-way along this lane there stands all that is left of Moon's Cross. This consists of a short section of an octagonal shaft fixed in a square socket-stone measuring about three feet three inches along each side. The corners of the socket-stone have been rounded off. Each of the eight faces of the shaft is about eight inches wide, i.e. it is about forty eight inches in circumference. This gives the impression that Moon's Cross must have been an imposing monument when it was intact. Nothing is known about how it came to be damaged but it was in its present condition when Ormerod described it in 1874. The cross is probably in its original position. South Zeal has a good village cross and it too, we shall visit later.

Cross at Fitz's Well.

Our exploration now takes us west, along the A.30 road to the town of Okehampton about three miles away. We turn left at the cross-roads in the centre of the town, into George Street and follow the road along southward and uphill out of the town. Soon, the road crosses a railway bridge and then makes a sharp turn to the right. A couple of hundred yards beyond the turn, the next cross comes into view, on the right of the road. This cross stands adjacent to a little wayside pool called Fitz's Well to which the cross seems to draw attention. The cross as we now see it is not complete, it was clearly once much taller. It is now about three feet tall, rectangular in section and measures twenty inches across the arms. A small piece has been broken off one arm. A cross eight inches long by six inches wide is incised between the arms.

Crossing tells us that in his day, there was a folk-story current which said that the cross was erected by a man and his wife, who, having been misled by the pixies and lost their way, found the spring and having drunk the water discovered that the spell was now lifted and that they were able to continue their journey. Crossing points out that this is merely a variation of the story told of another Dartmoor monument, Fice's Well, near Princetown, where there is no cross. Whether or not the pixies were involved, there seems to be little doubt that the same person was concerned in embellishing the two wells, Fitz and Fice are merely Devonshire variations of the same name. The person credited with this activity was one Sir John Fitz who lived at Tavistock in the 16th century. Fice's Well near Princetown bears the date 1568 which seems about right. But 1568 is very late for the erection of a roadside cross, even to mark a well and it seems likely that the cross is older than that. Here, Crossing has a possible explanation. He recalls that an even older authority (W.B . Bridges' *Account of the Barony and Town of Okehampton,* first published in 1839) quotes a tradition that the cross was brought to the well from St. Michael's Chapel at Halstock. This medieval chapel seems to have disappeared as early as the 15th or 16th century and only the scantiest traces can now be seen, about a quarter of a mile east of Fitz's Well. It could be that the broken cross was brought from the ruined chapel to mark the position of the well during the time that Sir John Fitz was Lord of the Manor of Meldon and owner of Okehampton Park.

We now return to Okehampton and follow the A.30 south-west for about three miles until we come to the place where it is crossed by the A.386 on Sourton Down, just outside the village of Sourton. A few yards to the south of the cross-roads, standing in the hedge by the side of the A.386 is a very interesting cross. This is a tall specimen, over 8 feet high and of rectangular section. The arms are very short and the head above the arms expands slightly upwards. The shaft of this cross bears an inscription which runs in three lines downwards. There has been much conjecture about the reading of this inscription and all that Crossing could make of it was that it included the letters INCID. But a more modern authority* has stated that it probably reads PRINCIPI IURIVOCI AUDETI, together with a chi-rho, the symbol of Christianity. This seems to be a personal name preceded by a title of authority. It is now more or less accepted that this stone was originally an early Christian memorial stone, perhaps of the 6th century and that later it was turned into a wayside cross. The cross, which is in good condition, has been defaced by having the letters H, T, O, & L cut upon its various faces. These are the initials of Hatherleigh, Tavistock, Okehampton and Launceston towards which the letters point the way. It will be remembered that a similar instance of vandalism was noted when Horsepit Cross at North Bovey was being described, It cannot be said whether or not the Sourton Down cross still occupies its original position.

---

* *The Kingdom of Dumnonia* by Susan M. Pearce, page 28 and plate 22d. Published by the Lodenek Press, 1978. A similar stone, which has not been turned into a cross, can be seen in Lustleigh Church. This bears the inscription DATUIDOCI CONHINOCI FILIUS, i.e. DATUIDOC SON OF CONHINOC.

Chapter 9

Wayside crosses in the Moretonhampstead and Bovey Tracey areas.

The area we are now about to investigate is not particularly well furnished with wayside crosses. This may be because over the centuries the countryside has been cultivated to a much greater extent than in other places around Dartmoor. In such districts stone crosses were at greater risk, firstly, because of their utilitarian value — for gateposts etc., and secondly because in some circumstances they were a nuisance, for example when a lane needed to be widened. However, there are a few specimens which ought not to be ignored, so we will now proceed to visit them.

Our first call is at Moretonhampstead which has an interesting village cross which will be dealt with later. From the centre of the village we take the Chagford road and then take the first lane on the right beyond the hospital. Soon we take a left fork and having passed Howton Farm see our cross on the right of the road a couple of hundred yards further on. This is Linscott Cross (anciently spelt Lynscott). It is a badly battered specimen, standing about five and a half feet tall. The head of the cross and one arm are missing and it is obvious that it has at some time been used as a gatepost. An incised cross eleven inches by seven has been cut upon its face. It seems that Ormerod knew nothing of this cross, at least he does not mention it. Crossing tells us that in his day it was rescued from its position as a gatepost and erected by the roadside. When Masson Phillips wrote in 1937 it was still standing. In about 1957 I noticed that it had fallen and reported the fact. Soon afterwards it was re-erected where it now stands.

At Linscott Cross an ancient track goes off through the fields to the north and connects with a lane coming up from Moretonhampstead and making for Fingle Bridge on the Teign. Beyond the bridge the road continues and links with a network of lanes coming in from Drewsteignton, Cheriton Bishop and numerous other places. To reach Fingle Bridge one had to descend a very steep zig-zag track which falls through the woods beyond Cranbrook Castle (a prehistoric fortification) to reach the river. In the woods, at an intersection of the main track with a subsidiary one, stands a stone pillar, more or less square in section which has a cross incised upon it. The stone is about three feet tall and the cross measures fourteen inches by ten. Ormerod mentions this stone and so do Crossing and Masson Phillips. It is clearly of considerable antiquity and probably replaces an even older waymark. It seems never to have been given a name.

Before leaving the vicinity of Moretonhampstead, it might be as well to mention two other objects in the vicinity. Standing on Mardon Down, a piece of open common about two miles NE of Moretonhampstead, is a stone pillar about six feet tall. This is variously called the Headless Cross and the Maximajor Stone. It seems unlikely that this ever was a cross, there is certainly no evidence that it was. Possibly it is a prehistoric menhir left over from the Bronze Age. On the other hand the pillar is surprisingly regular in shape as though a mason had tidied it up. Careful examination will bring to light the fact that the stone bears an incised bench mark. It might be that the surveyors engaged in the early 19th century Ordnance Survey could find nowhere permanent nearby to accommodate their bench mark and erected this stone for the purpose. Who knows?

Crossing (1902) and Masson Phillips (1937) both mention a cross, which when they wrote, was to be seen near Elsford Farm on the road from Hennock to Moretonhampstead. Crossing describes this cross as being only thirty-three inches tall and the same across the arms. Masson Phillips says that only the head portion of the cross was present and that one arm was broken, I have completely failed to find this cross after a number of careful searches and enquiries spread over the years between 1965 and 1982.

Another mysterious (but not quite so elusive) fragment of a cross is to be found built into the parapet wall of Budleigh Bridge, about a mile from Moretonhampstead on the Bovey Tracey road. This consists of the head only of a cross, the limbs of which expand outwards. The head bears the date 1911 incised upon it in very irregular characters. This cross is not mentioned by Ormerod or Crossing and I think it clear that they knew nothing of it. Masson Phillips first mentioned it in 1959, it having been reported to him by the Devon County Roads Engineer. He remarks that the cross appeared rather freshly cut and that the date upon it (which he read as 1711) would be very late if it were the date of its erection.

However, early in 1982 the walls of Budleigh Bridge were rebuilt and the cross was removed so that this could be done. I was thus enabled to minutely examine the cross. I found that it is very roughly cut and that the stone bears no evidence of weathering. The date upon it is undoubtedly 1911. Further and more important, the upper limb bears the unmistakeable half-round grooves made by the drill by means of which the stone was severed from its parent mass. This indicates that the cross was made no earlier than about 1800, the approximate date when this method of cutting granite was first used in this part of the world. It may well be much later than 1800, though the date 1911 seems more likely to be when the cross was first built into the bridge.

Where this cross came from no-one seems to know. It is clearly not ancient and I incline to the view that it is probably a throwout from a monumental mason's yard. It has now been built into the parapet of the bridge on the east side of the road, opposite where it used to be. Explorers who wish to visit Budleigh Bridge will not find it on the map under that name. The map calls it One Mill Bridge, probably a cartographer's mistake for One Mile Bridge—it is just about that distance from Moretonhampstead.

At the other end of the seven mile stretch of the A.382, just outside Bovey Tracey and on the south of the road, will be found "Bovey Stone". This is a short length of the chamfered shaft of a cross fixed in an octagonal socket-stone which is itself built into the garden wall of "Cross Cottage". An incised cross is cut upon the face of the shaft.

Both Crossing and Ormerod mention this fragment. Ormerod says that it was moved to its present position in 1815 when the road was being widened. It clearly originally stood nearby. He also recounts that annually on the first Monday after the 3rd of May the "Mayor" of Bovey Tracey (he was really the Portreave) used to ride around the cross and strike it with a stick. This ceremony probably had its origin in medieval times and was a reminder that Bovey Tracey had its market and such civic dignities as it possessed under a charter which came into force on the date in question, though why the old cross should have featured in the ceremony is not apparent. The original market charter is dated 18th July 1260, but there must have been others later.

Leaving for the time being a description of Bovey Churchyard Cross and Market Cross we make our way to the other end of the

Cross on North Bovey Green.

village. Here, standing on the edge of a green path near Challabrook Farm is a very battered ancient cross with a stange story attached. The Challabrook cross stands about five feet tall and is of very rude construction. One arm has been knocked off and the other is short. The head also appears to have been damaged long ago. The cross has obviously been used as a gatepost. What appear to be incised crosses have been cut on each face between the arms. A brass plate has been fixed to the shaft of the cross and an inscription on this plate reads: "This old cross once marked the grave of a Royalist officer who fell near here in 1645 when Cromwell's troops defeated the Royalists. A.J.W. 1923."

Both Ormerod and Crossing refer to this cross but it is clear from their comments that neither had seen it when they wrote. Masson Phillips, writing in 1937 describes the cross as we see it to-day. He comments that the inscription on the brass plate is "wholly fanciful". However, Armitage Hargraves in her charming little book *"Bovey Tracey History and Legend"* published in 1968 goes a little more deeply into the question. She says that William Ellis, who was born at Bovey Tracey in 1804, wrote about Bovey Tracey at various times and his writings were published in the South Devon Weekly Express in 1883. Ellis had heard the story of the cross being used as a memorial at the grave of a Royalist officer. He even gives the officer's name — Langstone, but one cannot help thinking that this was the description of the cross rather than the name of the deceased. However that may be, I cannot agree that the inscription on the cross is "wholly fanciful". It is of course incapable of proof, one way or the other. But to me nothing could be more natural or likely than that the comrades of a young officer who had been tragically killed in a skirmish should press into service an old wayside cross found along one of the several tracks which must have traversed Bovey Heathfield in the 17th century. Or it may have been done by Royalist sympathisers when the tide of the battle had rolled on. We shall never know. By the way, the initials A.J.W. on the brass plate are those of the late Mr. A.J. Wyatt who was deeply versed in local history.

Dunstone Cross as it was prior to 1981.

Chapter 10

Wayside crosses in the Widecombe-in-the-Moor area

The civil parish of Widecombe-in-the-Moor to-day includes within its boundaries the ecclesiastical parishes of Widecombe and Leusdon. Formerly it was a single parish whose area extended over more than 10,000 acres, much of which is wild moorland country. On the west Widecombe has a common boundary with the parish of Lydford and consequently with the Forest of Dartmoor. As early as the 13th century some at least of the people living on the ancient farms in the Forest were accustomed to use Widecombe parish church as their own instead of making the long, arduous and sometimes dangerous journey to Lydford. The Bishop of Exeter's authority for the dwellers at Babeny and Pizwell, both farms within the Forest, to do this is dated 1260. It is unlikely that the inhabitants of these farms were the only ones accorded this privilege; indeed, until within living memory it was customary for the residents of Hexworthy and Huccaby to do so also. This is exemplified by the existence of the famous Coffin Stone. This is a block of granite which lies alongside a green path which cuts off the great loop in the road that connects Dartmeet with places like Widecombe, Poundsgate, Leusdon and Ashburton. Upon the Coffin Stone the coffins of those on their way to burial at Widecombe churchyard used to be set down whilst the bearers rested half way up the long steep hill. The initials of some whose remains rested here will be found cut upon the stone. Several small crosses are also incised upon the stone. It will be noticed also that the stone is now in two halves, although it was obviously once a single slab. This is accounted for by a folk-story which recounts that on an occasion "long ago" when the coffin of a particularly wicked person had been set down upon the stone the Almighty demonstrated his indignation by sending a thunderbolt which destroyed the coffin and its contents and split the stone in two.

In so large a parish with so many scattered farms and hamlets, all sending worshippers to the parish church, to say nothing of licensees from outside, it is not surprising that several paths, designated "Church Paths" should exist in the parish. What is

Ouldsbroom Cross.

surprising is the fact that there are so few wayside crosses surviving to mark the tracks across the commons and through the lanes. To the best of my knowledge there are but four such crosses and I know of no tradition claiming the existence of others within the parish.

The first of the surviving crosses to be described is Ouldsbroom Cross. This stands near the intersection of the road which runs up Dartmeet Hill with a lane on the left which if followed takes the wayfarer to Widecombe by way of Ponsworthy. Ouldsbroom Cross has been vary badly treated. In Crossing's day it stood at Town Farm, Leusdon, doing duty as a gatepost. It was still in the same position when Masson Phillips wrote in 1937. The cross was restored to its present and probably original position in the 1950's. The cross is a tall one, nearly six feet tall I should think, and rude as to construction. To facilitate its use as a gatepost, both arms were knocked off and are still missing. According to Crossing this desecration took place in 1825, the cross being conveyed to the farm, which is about two miles distant, on a sledge drawn by four oxen. The place where the cross stands is also named Ouldsbroom Cross and a farm of the same name is about a quarter of a mile away to the east. The Coffin Stone is also about a quarter of a mile distant, to the SW, about a hundred yards south of the road. There is no doubt in my mind that Ouldsbroom Cross stands in its proper position, marking the path to Widecombe church.

From Ouldsbroom Cross we take the Widecombe lane. Having passed through the ancient and beautiful hamlet of Ponsworthy we mount the steep hill to the north. At the top of the hill, we take a lane on the left and this brings us to another ancient and picturesque place, Jordon, where there is a thatched manor house and an old mill. The road passes through the farmyard in front of the Jordan Manor and then begins to rise. This brings us in about a quarter of a mile to a cross-roads and here we find our next cross. The cross stands on the grass verge near the road junction. It has no formal name and is usually referred to as the cross near Drywells, the name of a nearby farm. This is a fine specimen, carefully shaped and it has been equally carefully restored. Crossing does not mention the Drywells Cross and it seems he knew nothing of it. When Masson Phillips wrote in 1937, the head only of this cross was built into the roadside wall near where it now stands, the shaft was missing. When I first began to take an interest in these matters in

Cross near Drywells.

the early 1950's I went to look for the cross and found that it had been removed from the wall and was lying on the roadside verge. There it remained for some considerable time and then it disappeared. I searched for it and found it lying on a rubbish dump inside a field some little distance away. I reported the facts to the Dartmoor Preservation Association and in 1967 the restoration took place. This consisted of mounting the head upon a replacement shaft which had been found in the grounds of a house named "Crichel" at Totnes. The restoration was carried out under the supervision of Mr Masson Phillips and is a decided success. As restored the cross stands about five feet six inches tall and measures about 20 inches across the arms. The replacement shaft which tapers slightly is octagonal in section and thus matches the head which has the unusual feature of being chamfered all round the arms and upper limb. On the face of the cross a rectangular socket has been cut. This is about six inches long by two inches wide and an inch deep. The exact purpose of this socket seems to be unknown but it is not unlikely that it was designed to accommodate an image, perhaps of the Crucifixion or something similar, carried out in a contrasting material, possibly marble or alabaster. There are other examples of crosses with similar features to be found in Devon. The point is I suppose that in the days of the iconoclasts it would be easy enough to lever out of its socket and destroy such an image. To break up and destroy a massive granite cross-head would demand much more effort and energy. It seems unlikely that the Drywells cross has been moved far over the centuries; its original purpose was probably to mark the cross roads where the Church path to Widecombe from Jordan (one of Widecombe's ancient manors formerly known as Dewdon) met a similar path coming from the north-western sector of the parish. The paths are still there to-day, except that they are now mostly lanes.

To find our next cross we follow the road from Drywells Cross north and east towards Widecombe. We do not go as far as the village however. The lane we are following soon breaks out into open moorland on Dunstone Down and at a point just about a mile from Drywells Cross we find a moorland track going off to the left (north) along the ridge of Hameldon. This great whale-backed ridge of high ground extends northward for nearly four miles from Widecombe and provides one of the easiest and most invigorating walks to be found in this part of Dartmoor. The track just described is joined after about three-quarters of a mile by another which converges upon it from the right. Soon after this the track forks, the left-hand branch going off down the side of Hameldon into the valley below. This is the ancient Church-path connecting the farms in the Forest around Postbridge with their adopted church. The main track continues northward however and soon passes by a number of prehistoric cairns (barrows) which are ancient burial places. Many of these have given their names to the much more modern boundary stones which will be seen standing nearby; Broad Barrow, Two Barrows, Single Barrow are examples. There are other stones with other names to be found also, e.g. Blue Jug, Hameldon Beacon, Hameldon Old House. These all date from the middle of the 19th century when the Duke of Somerset was Lord of the Manor of Natsworthy, the boundary of which runs along the ridge. A few hundred yards to the north of Broad Barrow another stone will be seen standing by the side of the track. On closer examination this will be found to be a very short and battered cross. To make quite sure that you make no mistake it has an inscription cut upon it. This reads H.C. D.S. 1854 meaning "Hameldon Cross, Duke of Somerset."

Hameldon Cross stands rather less than four and a half feet tall and it is about two feet across at its widest. It has lost one arm and part of the head is missing also. Crossing tells us that about 20 years before he wrote, he met one of the men who had cut the letters and figures upon this and other boundary stones in the vicinity. There seems to be little doubt that the Duke of Somerset's masons utilised an ancient wayside cross as a boundary stone, but I do not think that it now stands in its original position. It is more likely that it originally stood at the intersection of the track we have followed so far with the old Church Path coming up from the west, some two miles to the south. It is noteworthy that many of the wayside crosses so far described stand at cross-roads or junctions of tracks.

We now retrace our steps and descend to the road which enters Widecombe from the south, i.e. from the direction of Ponsworthy. On reaching this road, at the foot of the steep hill which runs past the ancient farm of Southcombe, we turn right and in less than half a mile, take a lane on our left. A few yards down this lane we reach a tiny patch of greensward in front of a farm on the left and an ancient manor house on the right. The place is Lower Dunstone and the

Hameldon Cross.

Dunstone Cross.

manor house is Dunstone Court, the home of the Hamlyn family. On the green will be seen a large granite boulder and an ancient granite cross. Both are noteworthy and of local importance. The cross has only recently been restored to its proper place, having been removed by a former Vicar of Widecombe to a position in the vicarage garden at some date prior to 1860 after the cross had fallen down. It was brought back to Dunstone and re-erected as it now is in 1981 by the munificence of Miss M. Hamlyn. Dunstone Cross is a rather rude specimen and is much weathered. In its present form it stands rather less than three feet tall, though it was probably once taller. It stands on an improvised plinth. Whether it was originally a waymark or served some other purpose it is impossible to say.

The other object of interest at Dunstone is the granite boulder mentioned earlier. This is sometimes known as the Rent Stone and it is an historical curiosity. Close examination of this boulder will show that upon its upper surface are a number of shallow saucer-shaped depressions. It seems that in former times, the Lord of the Manor used annually to meet his tenants at this spot to receive their rent. To avoid infection from the coins with which they paid, when the Black Death was raging, the saucer shaped depressions were filled with vinegar—as a form of disinfectant— and the coins placed in the vinegar. Crossing tells us that this custom (perhaps without the vinegar) was revived in the late 19th century. That this is a very ancient place there can be no doubt. Dunstone was Dunestanetuna when Domesday Book was compiled (1086) and local people even to-day often spell it Dunstan. But whether the name of the place is a reference to the Rent Stone is uncertain, it may have meant no more than Dunstan's Farm.

About two miles ESE of the village of Widecombe, at the top of Widecombe Hill is a road junction known as Hemsworthy Gate. Here the road from Widecombe bends round to the left and goes off to Haytor, Bovey Tracey and Ilsington, whilst another road goes south to Ashburton. Local people call this road junction White Gate, because many years ago a white gate spanned the road, cutting off the commons of Widecombe from those of the neighbouring parish of Ilsington. The gate has given way to a modern cattle-grid but the massive granite gate-posts still lie by the roadside at the junction. Also near the same spot is an erect pillar of granite about three and a half feet tall which on three separate faces bears the letters A.B. & M., signifying that the letters face towards

Ashburton, Bovey Tracey and Manaton respectively. Forty yards or so to the south of the cattle-grid, on the outside of the angle formed by the road-side wall where it meets another wall coming down from the SE is another granite pillar. This is about three and a half feet tall and it bears an incised cross and the letters R.M. This stone is always known as Stittleford's Cross; it is a boundary stone marking the limits of the Manor of Dunstone, referred to earlier in this chapter. Crossing was told that the initials R.M. were those of Rawlin Mallock, an 18th century Lord of the Manor.

The real significance of the cross cut upon Stittleford's Cross is not known. It may have been no more than an attempt to protect the stone from depredators, in continuance of a much older custom. On the other hand, the cross, together with the name of the stone may indicate that a true cross once stood at this spot, perhaps marking the track that preceded the road and the nearby junction. Where the name Stittleford comes from is a mystery though a clue may lie in the fact that a little over a mile away to the west, also within the Manor of Dunstone, is an ancient farm called Chittleford. Whether the two are connected in some way is at present unknown. The fact that this boundary stone bears a name at all is an interesting example of the local custom of giving such stones personal names. The custom is also applied to cross-roads.*

Stittleford's Cross lies at the north-western foot of Rippon Tor, the summit of which is only about a quarter of a mile away. A walk of about four hundred yards along the Ashburton road will bring us to the site of New House, formerly a moorland inn. There is no building here now, just a pleasant patch of greensward, some ancient thorn trees and a few old and ruined walls. The inn is said to have been burned down nearly 150 years ago. It served the traffic using the road from Ashburton to Moretonhampstead and no doubt fulfilled a useful purpose in those days of horse drawn vehicles and pack animals.

Almost opposite the site of New House is a small hunting gate which gives access to the enclosure in which Rippon Tor stands. A not too stiff climb of about a quarter of a mile brings us to the summit of Rippon Tor. This is far from being one of Dartmoor's highest tors, the summit is just over 1500 feet above sea level. But Rippon Tor is a frontier hill and from it tremendous views of the countryside around, including the South Hams and the sea, can be obtained. On the greensward on the north side of the tor, just a little below the summit, lies the reason for our visit here. This is a granite cross, cut in relief on the surface of the rock of which the tor is composed. The cross measures six feet eight inches in length and about twenty-seven inches across the arms. One of the arms is badly broken and so is the base of the shaft. It appears to be of great age.

Crossing describes the cross on Rippon Tor. He comments that it can never have been intended to set it up like other crosses and it would indeed have been difficult to have severed it from the parent rock. On the other hand Masson Phillips describes it as having been abandoned in the process of manufacture. Personally, I prefer Crossing's theory, but if this is correct the possible reasons for its presence on the tor present an interesting problem. Crossing quotes one of the older Dartmoor antiquaries, Spence Bate, who suggested that the cross was cut in more superstitious times when the symbol of the cross was held to be all powerful in dispelling evil forces from places where they held sway. On the summit of Rippon Tor are three immense cairns of stones, relics of Bronze Age times when the dead were habitually buried under such cairns. It is not unlikely that the medieval dwellers around the Moor found such burial sites frightening and the protection of the cross might well have been sought in such circumstances. Another possibility is of course that the cross was carved in memory of someone who died on or near the tor. But all is surmise, of evidence there is none.

* **Addendum:** It has very recently (January 1983) come to my notice that in an entry in the Islington Manor records under date 29th. October, 1835 a boundary stone which is almost certainly identical with Stittleford's Cross (see page 104) is referred to as Stentiford Cross. Why or when the change of name took place is unknown, as in the significance of the name, but the fact seems worth recording.

Wayside Cross in Gidleigh Churchyard.

Chapter 11

Crosses in Villages and Churchyards.

Very many towns and villages around the Dartmoor borders have ancient crosses standing at or near their centres and very many churchyards have crosses in them, other than gravestones. But this is not to say that these crosses are either the original and true village crosses or the ancient churchyard crosses. In the course of the last century or so many cases have arisen where an ancient cross has been found, often badly damaged or even fragmented, whose true identity was unknown and could only be conjectured at. In such a case the need for preservation was paramount and often the relic was erected either in the churchyard or in some other prominent place where it was thought it would be safe for ever—the cross in Harford churchyard is a case in point. So far this policy has worked very well, though at least one case is on record where a cross was removed to a safer site only to be moved again to a less suitable one later on. This will be described later.

We start our investigation of the crosses referred to above at Bovey Tracey, from whence we shall proceed clockwise around Dartmoor, making such deviations as may be necessary from time to time.

Bovey Tracey: The Town Hall at Bovey Tracey stands at the junction of Fore Street and Mary Street and adjacent to the building will be found the town's War Memorial. This takes the form of a large and imposing cross which is in fact the ancient Market Cross upon which the war memorial inscriptions are superimposed in bronze. The cross consists of a large square pedestal of modern stonework, octagonal at the top. This carries the plinth of an octagonal step with a projecting top edge which supports another octagonal step which is cased in bronze and bears the inscriptions. Above this is the original ancient socket-stone, square at the base and octagonal above and this carries the ancient shaft, which is about eight feet tall. This tapers upwards and is square at the base but octagonal above. Fixed upon it is a modern head, the limbs of which expand outward. A circlet of stone links the head and shaft. The new head was provided in the mid-nineteenth

Churchyard Cross, Bovey Tracey.

century. It was the gift of the Vicar of the parish, the Hon. Canon Courtenay. The cross was moved from its original position nearby at about the same time to make way for the new Town Hall.

From Bovey Town Hall we make our way up the hill to the church of St. Peter, St. Paul and St. Thomas of Canterbury. Apart from saying that to my mind this is one of Devon's most beautiful churches I shall not attempt any description of the church. Readers may like to know however that the old story of Bovey Tracey Church being one of those built as a penance by William De Tracey because of his part in the murder of St. Thomas a'Becket is unlikely to be true. William De Tracey came from a different branch of the family from that which provided the Lords of the Manor of Bovey Tracey.

In the part of the churchyard bordering the road, will be found a stately cross in what at first glance appears to be surprisingly good condition. Closer examination however reveals that only part of the cross is original, much new material having been incorporated. Crossing, quoting Ormerod, tells us that in the 19th century the then Lord Courtenay (later Earl of Devon) found the remains of the ancient churchyard cross in use as a step at the churchyard gate. The fragments consisted of part of the shaft and one arm. A very careful and successful restoration followed and the cross was then set up near the east end of the church. However, the cross was twice thrown down, one suspects as part of the conflict which troubled the Church of England at that time and eventually the cross was removed to Powderham Castle. In 1849 Canon Courtenay (a kinsman of the Earl of Devon) became vicar and the cross was then brought back and set up where we now see it. As Crossing says ". . . we see what good results a careful and judicious restoration may effect".

Manaton: The crosses to be found in the villages of Lustleigh and North Bovey have already been described in an earlier chapter which dealt with wayside crosses and it is now time to visit yet another charming border village of the same character as the two just mentioned—Manaton. This is another beautiful and ancient place, the centre of a large parish endowed with extensive commons bordering the Forest and containing many objects of great interest. These include Bowerman's Nose (once thought to be a Druidical rock idol), Jay's Grave, a suicide's grave with a famous story attached to it, and Grimspound, a Bronze Age village containing twenty four hut circles.

The parish church of St. Winifred, Manaton is to be found adjacent to the village green, round which are clustered the church and the ancient Church House, the Rectory and the buildings which were once the inn (The Half Moon) and the school and school-house, all now in private occupation. Embowered as it is by great trees and surrounded by picturesque buildings, Manaton Green presents as complete a picture of rural peace and charm as one can hope for. The church itself is well worth a visit on its own account and as the churchyard contains a cross with a most interesting story attached, our visit will be well repaid.

To find the cross we are seeking it is necessary to enter the churchyard from the green via the lych gate. We then walk along the path which leads us past the south door of the church when we see the cross ahead of us, close to a handgate giving access to a footpath beyond. The great majority of churchyard crosses, in Devon at least, are somewhat more formal in appearance and more carefully worked than most wayside crosses. Not so the one we now see before us. This is a tall cross, rather more than six feet high. It consists of a rough shaft of granite, more or less rectangular in section, with extremely short arms, one of which is almost completely missing, having been broken off. A cross with equal arms has been incised upon the face of the cross, between the arms. Looking at this cross, one realises that this is another of those where the mason has done the absolute minimum of work to achieve the appearance of a cross—in other words it is typical of many crosses to be found along the wayside or marking tracks across the moor. But an examination of the socket-stone in which the cross stands produces a surprise, for this turns out to be something very different. This socket-stone is square and carefully worked; the top edges have been chamfered and moulded and it is clearly a piece on which considerable care and skill has been expended by the mason. There is obviously a mystery here and the explanation is provided by the fascinating true story which follows.

In the year 1841, a new Rector came to take charge of Manaton parish. This clergyman's name was John C. Carwithen and it seems that his family had some considerable connection with the parish since he was the eighth of his name to hold the office. Be that as it may, it is clear that Mr. Carwithen did not find everything to his liking in his new parish. In particular, he found that the members of his flock had a peculiar custom of which he did not approve. This consisted of a ritual through which they went whenever someone had died and was to he buried in the churchyard. When this happened, before the interment took place, the deceased, in his coffin, was carried three times round the chruchyard cross. Clearly the rector found this custom objectionable, perhaps superstitious or irreligious and one supposes that he made some attempt to dissuade those responsible from continuing it. He failed however, and being a determined person, took forceful action. One morning the villagers were surprised to discover that the churchyard cross, of which no description seems to have survived, had disappeared, only the socket-stone remaining. It is said that the rector was at once suspected, but whether he was actually questioned does not appear. Exhaustive search was made in every likely place, apparently it was suspected that the cross might have been buried nearby, but no trace of it could be found and eventually the hue and cry died down and the matter was more or less forgotton. It is not surprising perhaps that Mr. Carwithen stayed only seven years at Manaton—he clearly has not endeared himself to his people.

One day, in 1908, a local man whose name I have been unable to discover, was working in the church at Manaton, attending to the bells, I was told. At mid-day, having had his lunch, he went for a short walk along the lane near the church. He eventually came to a spot where a wall was carried across a stream upon a long post of granite. He noticed that the granite post had a cross cut in it at one end and on closer examination found that the post was indeed a cross, complete except for one arm, which had been broken off and was missing. The story of the missing churchyard cross was then remembered and the then rector, thinking that the newly found cross was the missing one, had it erected in the empty socket-stone in the churchyard where we see it to-day. The identification was faulty of course, the newly found cross is quite unlike the kind of cross that would have belonged to the carefully made socket-stone; in any case it does not fit, as examination will show. There is no doubt that the cross now standing in Manaton churchyard originally came from some track or lane nearby where it acted as a waymark. It is equally true that the real Manaton churchyard cross has yet to be found, if it has not been utterly destroyed. For many years I have nourished an ambition that it should be I who found it and in furtherance of this ambition I still scrutinise every granite gate-post I see!

Oddly enough, Ormerod, writing in 1874, seems to have known nothing about the Manaton churchyard cross and its strange history. But Crossing, in 1902, tells the story up to date and Masson Phillips completes the saga in 1937 except for some of the fine detail which is my own contribution.

Widecombe-in-the-Moor: Widecombe too has the remains of its churchyard and village crosses. The latter, only the base of which remains, stood in the open space in front of the old Church House and close to the lych gate giving access to the churchyard. The base consists of two steps. It is octagonal in shape and a plinth about six inches high runs round the bottom. The base is something over eight feet in diameter and stands about three and a half feet high. the cross itself is missing, as it was in Ormerod's day and an ancient yew tree is growing inside the base.

To the south of the base just described is another similar raised and kerbed area, but much larger. Until recently this housed a great elm tree but it died of Dutch Elm disease about three years ago and had to be felled. Records exist which appear to show that the elm was planted in 1822 and that the yew first planted in the cross-base dated from 1793. No information seems to be available about the fate of the village cross, nor have I been able to find out what was the original function of the second, larger raised area where the elm stood. It was clearly very carefully constructed and has the appearance of having been intended to serve as a platform, perhaps for village functions and the like.

Passing through the lych gate we make our way to the south door of the church. Here we see what may be the ancient churchyard cross, or perhaps but less likely, the village cross. It has been restored from a fragmentary condition and now stands in front of the door, just clear of the footpath. The cross as restored, stands about 6 feet tall and measures about two feet across the arms. The shaft is square at the base and octagonal above. It stands in an apparently ancient socket-stone which also is square at the base and octagonal above. Close examination of the cross shows that it is composed of a number of fragments, carefully brought together, and that one arm is a replacement.

Ormerod tells us that when he wrote, only the base and part of the

112

shaft stood in the present position. He adds that part of the shaft and the head of a cross were built into the wall of the churchyard; he could not say whether or not this was part of the churchyard cross. Crossing also describes the broken shaft and socket-stone standing near the south door and the remains built into the wall. As he and Ormerod both say that both arms were in view, one wonders what happened to make it necessary to provide the present cross with one new arm. Or were they perhaps part of two different crosses? If this is the case then something still remains to be found at Widecombe. I do not know the date of the restoration of this churchyard cross, but Crossing, in an addendum, says it took place prior to 1902.

Don't leave without looking into the church, magnificent in its simplicity. In particular, look for the wooden tablets setting out in doggerel the story of the great Widecombe thunderstorm of 1638 and how the Devil visited the church on that occasion.

Buckland-in-the-Moor: This tiny village, really only a hamlet but famous for its beauty, even in beautiful Devon, boasts two crosses, both in a sorry state. The base of the first will be found just outside the south gate of the church. It consists of a large octagonal pedestal of one stage with a projecting top edge. The pedestal is over ten feet in diameter. A tree grows in the centre, (Crossing says it was a sycamore but the present occupant is an oak), and there is a memorial plaque commemorating the planting of the tree in 1935. Nearby, acting as the coping stones on top of the churchyard wall are the upper part, of the shaft and the arm of a cross of octagonal section. The fragment of the shaft is about two feet long and the cross when complete would have been about twenty-six inches across the arms. One arm is shorter than the other by about three and a half inches. There seems to be little doubt that we see here the remains of Buckland's village cross. This ancient place was part of the estate of Torre Abbey and the monks of Torre must have been closely associated with the church. Perhaps the cross was a preaching station erected before the church was built some time in the 12th century.

To find Buckland's second cross we leave the church and descend the steep hill to the south. As we walk down the hill we have on our right hand the high wall of Buckland Court. About half way along the wall diligent search will bring to light the shaft and one arm of a cross; built into the wall in such a way that one shoulder protrudes.

This is a very rude cross and it is badly damaged, one arm being missing. A square hole has been cut in the shaft which gives the impression that it has been in use as a gatepost at some time. Where this cross came from no-one knows. My own feeling is that it formerly did duty as a waymark along some moorland track (it seems to be that kind of cross) and was brought from the moor with a load of other stones when the wall was being built, probably in the late 18th or early 19th century.

Ashburton: This little town, famous as a Stannary Town and one of the principal centres of the once all important woollen trade, is steeped in history. Its origins go back into antiquity; it was part of the enormous estates of the Bishops of Exeter before the Conquest and it already had a market before the end of the 12th century.*

For all its history and charm, Ashburton can boast only one ancient cross, though the records seem to tell us that formerly there were more. In the records of the Borough Court for 1807 there is a reference to the Market Cross. This probably stood adjacent to the Market Hall, at the junction of North Street with East and West Streets. The Hall was demolished in 1848 and no doubt the cross went with it. There are references on a map dated 1605 to "Benecrosse" and "Shortacrosse". These both apparently stood along the road from Ashburton to Buckland-in-the-Moor and the whereabouts of neither is now known. But—is it not possible that the cross built into the wall of Buckland Court is one or other of these?

The one cross that does survive is St. Gudula's Cross. This stands beside the Old Totnes Road, a turning off West Street, adjacent to the ancient Gulwell. St. Guldula it seems was a Flemish saint and parton of the weak-sighted. The water of Gulwell was thought to be beneficial to those with ailing eye-sight and that is given as the reason for the presence of the cross by the well. There are those however who deny St. Gudula any property in this cross and prefer the claims of one St. Gulwall, a Celtic Holy Man of the 6th century. It appears that he travelled widely in this part of the world and it is thought that he may have blessed the well to give it healing properties. However this may be, many elderly people in the town

---

*For further information about Ashburton see "Ashburton. The Dartmoor Town" by Francis Pilkington, 1978.

remember going to the well as children and there filling bottles with the holy water for future use.

The cross as we see it to-day stands about eight feet tall. It consists of a shaft which is square at the base and octagonal above; only part of it is original and upon this is set the ancient head and arms. The ancient socket-stone is missing. This was hollowed out and turned into a trough many years ago. It formerly stood under a pump in the town but when I went in search of it in 1966 I discovered that it had been broken up about ten years earlier and used as filling for the well when the pump was removed.

In Crossing's time the cross itself was missing from its accustomed place. At that time it was in two parts at Gulwell Farm about a quarter of a mile away. The shaft then formed part of the upping-stocks in the farmyard whilst the head and arms were in a farm building where they served as a support for a cider vat.

In 1933 the cross was restored and presented to the Parish of Ashburton. A plaque nearby states that the cross is probably 14th century in date and that it was removed prior to 1510.

Holne: The village of Holne lies rather more than three miles to the west of Ashburton, among the hills above the valley of the Dart. It is a splendid example of a Dartmoor border village and well merits a visit quite apart from the fact that it possesses an ancient and unusual cross. The cross in question will be found in the churchyard just to the south of the church. It stands at the head of a grave in which lies buried a former Vicar of Holne, the Revd. John Gill who died in 1917 at the age of 90 having been Vicar of the parish for 59 years. The Vicar's widow and his son, who died in 1884, are also buried at the same spot.

The cross is four feet three inches tall and measures twenty seven inches across the arms. The shaft and arms are octagonal in section, the shaft tapering slightly upward. Both shaft and arms have a convex moulding bounded by incised lines running the length of the shaft and along the arms, giving the cross a striking appearance. Both arms have been broken off and repaired with very carefully matched replacements. There are three holes, also repaired, in the shaft, indicating that the cross has at some time been used as a gatepost. The cement used to repair the damage is now beginning to crumble and the defects are much more noticeable than they used to be. The cross stands upon a modern pedestal of three steps.

Crossing, quoting Robert Burnard's "Dartmoor Pictorial Records" tells us that the cross at Holne was found doing duty as a gatepost. It was acquired by a resident, Mrs Bridget Lane, who died in 1870, and it was she who caused the cross to be repaired and set up in the churchyard. As this restoration took place before 1870 and as the Vicar's son did not die until 1884, it is apparent that the cross was not set up as a gravestone; it seems that the Gill family grave was so positioned in relation to the cross as to form an association between the two. The grave is surrounded by a low kerb, with inscriptions identifying the occupants of the grave. Growing near the cross is a splendid old yew tree. This also is mentioned by Crossing. It still flourishes despite the fact that it is quite hollow.

Near the cross just described stands the village War Memorial. This takes the form of a handsome modern cross, about eight feet high, which is mounted upon a pedestal of seven stages, the upper five of which are octagonal in shape. One of these stages, the fifth counting upwards, is an ancient socket-stone which has been hollowed out to form a trough. It once rested in the church and according to Masson Phillips it used to be pointed out as the font in which Charles Kingsley was baptised. (Kingsley's father was Vicar of Holne and the writer was born in the Vicarage here). The socket-stone was incorporated in the War Memorial when it was erected after the first World War. Until the 1960's the memorial stood outside the churchyard, opposite the Church House Inn but was removed when the adjacent site was built upon. The socket-stone probably belonged to the ancient churchyard cross and it is quite likely that the cross standing by the grave is that cross.

Buckfast and Buckfastleigh: Making our way southward through the lanes from Holne, our next port of call is Buckfast Abbey. This magnificent modern church stands upon the site of a much earlier abbey, founded in 1018. The abbey has extensive and beautiful grounds to which the public are allowed generous access. In the grounds, just to the north of the abbey church, are two ancient stone crosses which are not really part of the abbey possessions but which have found refuge here in the absence of information as to their proper sites.

The first of the two crosses now under discussion will be found in the centre of a round flower bed to the right of the entrance as one comes in from the road. This is a most unusual cross and I cannot do better than to describe it in the words Masson Phillips used in his report in 1954. "The cross is of granite, rather crudely shaped. Its total length is four feet one and a half inches; width across arms one foot nine inches. Width of shaft at base one foot four inches and thickness about ten and a half inches. On each face it bears a cross outlined by incised lines, the shaft of which is prolonged downwards. In general shape and in the character of the incised crosses this little cross is quite unusual in Devon. Its original site is unknown but an ancient cross is said to have stood at Stidson Cross, not far from Great Palston." The cross incised on the west face has an extended or additional foot containing a small incised cross.

This cross was found at the farm entrance to Great Palston Farm, South Brent, about 1942. It was buried below ground and the head had been broken from the shaft but both portions were present and both were eventually unearthed and re-united. The cross was erected at Buckfast Abbey as being one way of securing the safety of a relic whose proper site was unknown.

Not far from the cross just described will be found another and very different specimen. This stands at the end of a low wall a few yards to the west of the first. It stands about thirty eight inches tall and the shaft and the one surviving arm are octagonal (hollow chamfered) in section. When complete the cross would have measured about twenty two inches across the arms. At the point where the missing arm has been broken off are two round holes which appear to indicate an attempt to repair the cross (probably in antiquity) by dowelling.

This cross was first described by Masson Phillips in 1937. He then reported that the cross lay buried under the garden patch in front of the window of the old Smithy at Moor Shop cross-roads about two and a half miles east of Tavistock (Sampford Spiney Parish). At that time it was intended to erect the cross by the roadside nearby, but the War caught up with events and to safeguard the cross it was presented by the owner, Mrs Calmady Hamlyn, to the monks of Buckfast who have been its guardians ever since. The original site of this cross is unknown, but the old Smithy, where it was found, stands on an ancient road connecting Okehampton and North Devon with Plymouth and Plympton and places in between, so it was probably not far from home when found. Another cross which may have been associated with this track will be described in a later chapter.

117

From Buckfast Abbey we now mount the steep hill to the west to visit the parish chruch of Buckfastleigh—Holy Trinity. To me this is a rather dull building; but it has the distinction of being the only Dartmoor border church which possesses a spire. Magnificent views of the Dart valley can be seen from the churchyard and there is also the strange little building which houses the tomb of Richard Cabell. He was the traditional "wicked squire" of former days and it is said that his tomb was enclosed to prevent him from getting out. He has also been identified with the Demon Hunter who with his hounds hunts the souls of wicked people across the Moor on dark nights.

But we have come here to discover an ancient cross and this we shall find in the churchyard, NE of the church. The cross marks an un-named grave close to the ornate tomb of a member of the Furneaux family. It stands three and a half feet tall and measures eighteen inches across the arms. No socket-stone is visible. The shaft and limbs are octagonal in section. The head has been broken off at some time and neatly repaired. This is quite a dainty little granite cross and has all the appearances of being a carefully made wayside cross.

Our only information about this cross comes from William Crossing. He says that some forty years before he wrote in 1902, the cross came into the possession of Mr. R.J. King who intended to set it up on Dartmoor, whence it had originally come. R.J. King, a notable local historian of the 19th century, formerly lived at Bigadon in Buckfastleigh parish. He moved away before his project to set up the cross could be effected and left the cross at Bigadon. Consequently, it came into the possesion of Lady Littler, the new owner of the property and it was she who utilised the cross as a gravestone on a grave, the name of whose occupant now seems to be unknown.

By the way, if you feel the need for exercise while in this part of the world, I suggest you make your way into Buckfastleigh itself. Park your vehicle in one of the carparks in the town and then make your way to the church via the flight of steps—nearly 200 of them—which take you up the hill from the east end of the town. Nearby are the famous Buckfastleigh limestone caves.

Wrangaton (Ugborough Parish): Making our way westward from Buckfastleigh our route takes us past the village of Dean Prior and the border town of South Brent. Neither of these places now boasts an ancient cross, although both Crossing and Masson Phillips tell us that South Brent once possessed what must have been a nice specimen. Crossing, writing in the Western Antiquary (Vol.2, 1882, P.100) tells us that until a few years prior to that date the cross stood in or near the Market Place in the town. After the Market House was demolished the cross was removed to a court behind the Anchor Hotel, where at the time of writing it was still lying. Writing later, in 1902, Crossing says that the cross had comparatively recently been broken up and used for building purposes. In some ways the 19th century was a surprisingly unenlightened period.

To find our next cross, we make our way through the border lanes to the hamlet of Wrangaton, which lies within the parish of Ugborough. Here, at a "T" junction a back road connecting South Brent with Bittaford is joined by a road coming up from the SE. Close to the cross-roads, on the western side is a thatched cottage and mounted upon the roadside wall of the cottage is the cross. It is a most unusual specimen and as I cannot better it I quote Masson Phillips' description verbatim. He says: "A massive monolithic cross, the shaft of oval section, very wide at the base and tapering upwards. Below the arms it narrows and then becomes rectangular in section, the arms are short and straight but their ends slope inwards, and the head tapers upwards. There is an incised cross on each face between the arms. The cross is set up on a modern rectangular socket-stone."

When Masson Phillips described this cross in 1937 it was standing on the lawn at Wrangaton House, near its present situation. The cross had been found at a nearby cross-roads where it was serving as a gatepost. He later reported (1959) that the cross had been removed from the lawn and was awaiting re-erection nearby. I first saw it in its present position in about 1960.

It is a pity that we have no knowledge of where this cross came from or what was its original purpose. It is so massive and so unusual in design that one is almost forced to think that it must have been more than usually important. But in the absence of information, we are left with conjecture and with the pleasing thought that it has at least been preserved to us.

Bickleigh: The village of Bickleigh occupies a position on the South-Western edge of Dartmoor and stands among some spectacularly beautiful countryside in the valley of the Plym, known locally as Bickleigh Vale. We have already visited the parish in search of wayside crosses marking the line of the Plympton Track and now make our way to the village itself to examine the village cross. This stands upon the green, adjacent to the church and is a particularly impressive specimen.

The first reference to the village cross at Bickleigh that I have found is by Crossing, in his book of 1902. Here, he describes the cross as being of striking appearance, which it certainly is. The cross is mounted upon a calvary of two square steps, the lower one six feet square, formed from granite slabs. The socket-stone of the cross is also square and has a moulded upper edge. The socket-stone is modern and supports a modern rectangular shaft which tapers upwards. Surmounting the shaft is an ancient head of most unusual design which is fitted with a collar at the point where it meets the shaft. the lower part of the head is square in section but becomes octagonal above. In the angles between the arms and the shaft, above and below, are spurs or crockets, somewhat blurred as to detail because of weathering or damage in the past. The cross in its entirety stands over 11 feet tall. Masson Phillips also described this cross in 1937 and expressed the opinion that the head was of a design unique in Devon. In a later paper he wrote that he now thought that the head of the cross was very likely an ancient gable cross from the church.

Little seems to be known about the history of Bickleigh cross or its restoration. It seems very likely that it was originally a preaching cross and that it now stands at or near its original position. The church was rebuilt in 1838 by Sir Ralph Lopes, an ancestor of the present Lord Roborough and it is not unlikely that the cross was restored at or about the same time.

Buckland Monachorum: This delightful village stands about one mile south of Buckland Abbey, with which it was formerly associated. Hence its name which means "the Book-land of the Monks", i.e. land held by virtue of a charter. Reference to this aspect has already been made in an earlier chapter. There are many ancient and beautiful buildings in and around the village and the church itself, dedicated to St. Andrew, is splendid. It was completely rebuilt about 1490 and is maintained in pristine condition by many loving hands.

Just inside the churchyard stands a tall and imposing cross which, an inscription tells us, was restored to commemorate Queen Victoria's Diamond Jubilee in 1898. Close examination of this cross will reveal that it contains much new material but also a considerable quantity of ancient stone. William Crossing tells us that the village cross at Buckland formerly stood on the opposite side of the road from the church. In the early or middle 19th century it seems the cross was pulled down to make way for the cottages which now occupy the site. The material from the pedestal of the cross was left lying nearby in the shape of a confused heap of large stones, says Crossing. The remains included the socket-stone, a very large fine specimen which is incorporated in the present cross.

Masson Phillips describes the Buckland cross. He points out that the original material was Roborough Down stone, whilst the shaft and head, which are replacements, are of granite. Both Crossing and Masson Phillips described the replacement head as being of the lantern type but the latter, in a later report (in 1979) points out that the lantern head had by then been removed because it was felt that it was dangerous and replaced by a head of more conventional shape. This new head is somewhat unusual in that it has been constructed in three separate sections. Nearby, also in the churchyard, is an octagonal granite shaft topped by an ancient sculpted capital of Roborough stone. This is now surmounted by a sundial. There is no evidence, but it is not unlikely that the capital once formed part of the cross just described.

Meavy: This is another western border village which in the past was deeply associated with the monks of Buckland Abbey. It too, and its church were part of their possessions and to-day it also has a restored village cross which almost certainly started out in life as a preaching cross.

We learn from Crossing that until the late 19th century all that was to be seen of Meavy's village cross was the base and pedestal, which stood where the cross now stands under the ancient oak tree on the village green. Apparently the cross had been destroyed many years earlier, but not completely, for in 1882 the then vicar found the octagonal shaft of the cross minus its head and arms, doing duty as a gatepost in a field nearby.

It appears that it was not until 1895 that the cross was fully restored and by then some additional material, part of the original plinth, had also come to light.

Meavy's village cross as we see it to-day is a fine specimen. It consists of a massive pedestal of three octagonal steps, which contain much original material. This is surmounted by the original socket-stone, also octagonal, bearing the ancient shaft which has been fitted with a new head and arms. The complete cross must stand well over 11 feet tall.

As one surveys the scene around the village green at Meavy one cannot help being struck by the peaceful charm of the place. The combination of grey stone cross, ancient oak tree and green grass blends so completely with the background of granite church and ancient inn (The Royal Oak of course) as to bring a lump to the throat. The immense tree under which the cross stands is quite hollow and has been so for over a hundred and fifty years. There is a tradition—dating from at least 1826—that nine people once dined inside the tree. The Royal Oak Inn also is not without interest. The building is owned by the parish and the rent from it helps to relieve the rates—a splendid arrangement I think.

Sheepstor: The tiny village of Sheepstor stands on the very edge of western Dartmoor, indeed the open moor comes up almost to its doorstep. The village has a marvellous situation, overshadowed as it is by the massive bulk of Sheepstor (the tor itself) from which the village took its name in the 12th century, and alongside the placid waters of Burrator Lake. This is Plymouth's reservoir but enjoys the deserved reputation of being one of England's most beautiful man-made lakes.

The centre of the village is the church, a tiny granite gem which must be visited for its own sake. Just outside the churchyard, near the lych-gate, stands a beautifully proportioned granite cross which has to be examined carefully before it is realised that this too is a restoration.

When Crossing wrote in 1902, the base of the Sheepstor cross stood at the junction of two lanes, east of the church, whilst the cross itself, both arms of which had been broken off, stood in a field at Burrator serving as a rubbing post for cattle. In 1910 it was decided to restore the cross to commemorate the coronation of King George the Fifth. It was fitted with two new arms and erected where it now stands. As we see it to-day the Sheepstor cross is a massive specimen of rectangular section with chamfered edges. The head

Cross in Sheepstor churchyard.

and arms expand outwards. On each face and extending down the shaft is a cross cut in relief. The socket-stone in which the cross stands seems not to be the original and what became of this is unknown.

The first origins of the Sheepstor cross are uncertain, it may of course have been the village cross from the beginning. It seems to have been known as Rumon's or St. Rumon's Cross at one time but no reason for this is forthcoming. As already stated in an earlier chapter, Richard Hansford Worth advanced the interesting theory that this cross might be the original Smallacumba Cross, one of the boundary marks of the Buckland Abbey lands, which is known to have stood on Ringmoor Down not far from Sheepstor village. The reasons behind Worth's theory are unknown to me.

Sheepstor churchyard contains one or two objects of interest, including the family tombs of the Brooke family, the former White Rajahs of Sarawak, who made their home at Burrator, nearby. There is also another cross which provides a little mystery. This stands by a stile at the head of a steep flight of steps coming up from the ancient Playfield below. The cross has an octagonal shaft and this also has been fitted with two new arms very carefully matched to the shaft. Although this cross has been in its present position for a good many years, its origins seem to be unknown. Some authorities, including the Revd. Sabine Baring Gould have claimed that it was the original churchyard cross but there is no evidence of this and it is quite unlike any churchyard cross I have ever seen. It now serves as a handhold to help wayfarers over the stile—a very suitable function for the symbol of Christianity one might think. Near the door of the church is a circular granite slab with an incised cross within a circle cut upon it. This is not an ancient wheel-cross as some people have thought but the base of a domestic cheese-press—it is even fitted with a lip to direct the whey into the vat below. Built into the churchyard wall, on the outside facing east is the ancient holy well of St. Leonard, to whom it is thought the church itself is dedicated, though this is not absolutely certain. In the playfield, to the south of the church, is an iron ring to which the bull was tethered in the days when the barbarous sport of bull baiting was practised.

Sampford Spiney: We have already visited Sampford Spiney whilst following the Plympton track; this time we are here to examine the ancient cross which stands upon the green close to the church. The cross is about seven feet tall; it has a long tapering shaft which is square at the base and octagonal above. The arms are short in comparison to the shaft, being only about twenty inches across. The shaft is set in a socket cut in a large boulder. Crossing tells us that the cross formerly stood in the hedge nearby but was removed to its present free-standing position, presumably in the 19th century, by the then Lord of the Manor. Nothing more seems to be known of the history of this graceful cross, but from its appearance it seems likely that it was set up many centuries ago, perhaps to replace one which formed the original preaching cross before the church was built. Don't fail to visit the church at Sampford Spiney. To me it is one of the simplest, most peaceful and yet most beautiful to be found in the Dartmoor borderlands.

Peter Tavy: From Sampford Spiney one might have expected the trail to lead us to the nearby ancient and beautiful town of Tavistock. But Tavistock, interesting place though it is, has no cross to offer for our examination. We know from the writings of Mrs Bray and others that the town formerly had a market cross and also another which stood close to the holy well of St. John. Both these have gone, swept away in the name of improvement no doubt, though the cross near the well seems to have been in existence as late as 1846. Our next visit then will be to the village of Peter Tavy, which lies about three miles NE of Tavistock and three and a half NW of Sampford Spiney. The road to Peter Tavy from the latter place takes us via a cross roads called Moor Shop where, it will be recalled, one of the crosses now at Buckfast Abbey was found some years ago. Proceeding north from Moor Shop and about a mile beyond the cross roads a lane comes in from the right (east). This leads to a very ancient farm called Coxtor. Just before reaching the farm, a stone cross will be seen standing by the roadside on the right of the road, near a gateway. This cross stands only about four feet tall, and one arm is missing and the other is quite short. Examination will reveal quite distinctly that the cross has at one time been used as a gatepost, as the marks in the stone will show. In fact until about two years ago, it performed this function in the nearby gateway. It was then moved to its present and more appropriate position when the gateway was widened. Although this cross had obviously done duty as a gatepost for many years, Crossing does not mention it and one can only suppose that he did not know about it. Masson Phillips described it as it then was — in the gateway — in 1937. But it seems unlikely that it originally stood at its present location and my own opinion is that it probably marked the road along which we came via Moor Shop and that the cross now at Buckfast most likely served a similar purpose along the same road. An ancient inscribed stone giving distances to various places, including Plymouth, still stands along the same road between Peter Tavy and Moor Shop.

From Coxtor we make our way into Peter Tavy village, which is only about a mile and a quarter distant. This peaceful place with its ancient church and other buildings, with village green and stream running by provides just the setting for an ancient village cross. But alas, there is none. But Crossing tells us that this was not always the case. He says that several years before the publication of his book in 1902, he learned from a former sexton that a cross once stood near the churchyard gate. It was thought that the cross impeded the roadway and so it was dismantled and the stones forming the pedestal thrown on one side. What was probably the socket-stone of this cross can be seen acting as a coping stone on the churchyard wall and stones which may have been part of the pedestal lie nearby. The date of the destruction just described is uncertain but Crossing also says that in Miss Rachael Evans' "Home Scenes", a book published in 1846, there is a reference to a cross that formerly existed here.

In Peter Tavy churchyard, occupying a position to the left of the gate as one enters, is a grave surrounded by a stone kerb. On the kerb is an inscription which indicates that the grave is that of a member of the Fraser family. At the head of the grave is a granite cross which is an almost perfect replica of the Windypost (Beckamoor Cross to give it is proper name), which stands near Pew Tor, marking the line of the Abbot's Way. This cross is a modern copy, but so well has the mason done his work, including the weathering to be found on the Windypost, that it could well be mistaken for the genuine article, especially in years to come when the true facts could be difficult to come by.

Mary Tavy: Peter Tavy's sister parish, lies just across the River Tavy. As Crossing puts it, it is "one mile from tower to tower". Here, just inside the churchyard will be found the village cross. This may sound a trifle anomalous but the fact is that in 1880 the churchyard at Mary Tavy was extended so as to take in part of the open space beyond, upon which stood the village cross — and so it is. This is a handsome cross; it stands upon an ancient pedestal of three steps and upon this stands the ancient square socket-stone. The stocket-stone has a chamfered top edge and the sides are decorated with what appear to be flowers, carved in relief. The shaft, which is square at the base and octagonal above is rather less than five feet tall and bears a modern head and arms.

When Mary Tavy's cross lost its head is unknown, but writing in an addendum in 1940, Masson Phillips reported that since he first wrote in 1937, part of the original head had come to light. This now lies nearby. At the same time, Masson Phillips pointed out that whilst the pedestal and socket-stone (and the newly found portion of the head) are all granite, the shaft itself is of Roborough Down stone. The shaft is a trifle slender for the socket-stone and these discrepancies may indicate that we have here parts of two different crosses. Perhaps a replacement for the village cross was found necessary long ago.

William Crossing lived at Mary Tavy in his latter years and he and his wife lie buried in the churchyard here. In view of what we, and all Dartmoor lovers, owe him it would be a pity to leave without visiting his grave. This will be found east of the church. It was repaired and tidied up a few years ago by the Dartmoor Preservation Association and is now in presentable condition.

Sourton: This tiny border village (whose name by the way is always pronounced Sawton) stands astride the A.386 Okehampton to Tavistock road. It shares with its sister village of Bridestowe extensive commons on the western edge of Dartmoor and is an admirable jumping off place for exploring that part of Dartmoor lying in the vicinity of the Sourton Tors and the valley of the West Ockment river.

The little parish church of St. Thomas of Canterbury stands near the village green and is grey, venerable and beautiful in its own special way. Because of its dedication to Thomas a'Becket, the church has been thought to be one of those said to have been built by William de Tracey in expiation of his part in the murder of the archbishop, but there is no evidence that this is true.

Sourton is just the kind of place which one would expect to possess a village cross and indeed at one time this was the case.

Almost all that is left of the cross is the rectangular granite socket-stone which stands on the green near the road. This has a rectangular socket about nine inches square cut in it and in this is loosely fitted the stump of the shaft of the cross. This is about 18 inches long and circular in section. It terminates in a square tenon which exactly fits the socket. It will be noted that the break in the shaft is clearly of recent origin and that the break is scarred by a semi-circular groove made by the drill used to divide the shaft. When Crossing (and later Masson Phillips) wrote, only the the socket-stone was present. On making local enquiries, I discovered that the stump of shaft was found in a nearby building when renovation work was being carried out in 1980 or 1981. Unfortunately, the identity of the shaft was not realised until after is had been split but it is greatly to the credit of those responsible that the remaining section has been preserved. We now have to hope that the remainder of the cross will one day come to light.

Okehampton, South Zeal and South Tawton: From Sourton we make our way northward along the A.386 road to Okehampton. This ancient and attractive town would, one would think, be sure to have a cross to offer for our inspection. But no! Here again we find the same sad story of lack of interest in years gone by. It is truly extraordinary how many of the Dartmoor border towns once had town or market crosses which are missing to-day, or, if they are present, are reconstructions containing fragments of the original cross. The cases of Ashburton, South Brent and Tavistock have already been quoted and others are yet to come.

The town cross at Okehampton once stood in the centre of the town. Both Crossing and Masson Phillips refer to entries in a 17th century diary. The diary or journal was kept by one Richard Shebbeare, Mayor of Okehampton and refers to proclamations being read at "the Towne Crosse" in 1667 and 1696. Since then all is silence and to-day no trace of the cross seems to remain.

Leaving Okehampton by the A.30 road, we soon reach the village of Sticklepath. Just beyond the village we turn off to the left (north) and this quickly brings us to South Zeal. This is another attractive village which sits astride a road which was once the main road from Exeter to Okehampton and beyond. Now, the once important road is the village street and carries little through-traffic. In the centre of the village stands the village cross and close by a medieval chapel, dedicated to St. Mary. This was provided as a Chapel of Ease because the parish church at South Tawton is some distance away. Unfortunately, the chapel was rebuilt in the 18th century in a very solid but quite uninspiring style.

South Zeal's village cross however is a splendid specimen. It stands upon a pedestal of three square steps with projecting top edges. Upon this stands the massive square socket-stone into which is fitted a tall tapering shaft, square at the base and octagonal above, which is about nine feet tall. The shaft bears the ancient head and arms which are formed in one piece but separate from the shaft. It seems very likely that this cross was erected as a preaching station before the Chapel of Ease was built.

Both Ormerod and Crossing describe this cross in detail. Both relate how in the 1830's, a native of the village came home from America on a visit and restored the cross which apparently was in need of attention. Ormerod says that the person concerned was a Roman Catholic and that he restored the cross as an act of thanksgiving for the preservation of his life during a storm at sea. Crossing denies this part of the story. He says that the person concerned was one John Stanbury, who repaired the cross himself and as a memento of his visit carved his initials and the date on a stone which is incorporated in the base of the cross. His fellow villagers however, resented this piece of self-advertisement and erased the inscription. The marks caused by the erasure can still be seen. According to Crossing, Stanbury took umbrage at this and never again visited his native village. He died at Brooklyn, New York many years after the events described.

Whilst you are at South Zeal don't fail to have a look at its famous public house, the Oxenham Arms. This beautiful old building was once the Manor House of the Oxenham family, already referred to in connection with the legend of the White Bird of the Oxenhams. It dates at least from the early 16th century and parts of it may be much older. In one of the ground floor rooms is a prehistoric orthostat or menhir, left in situ when the house was built. At least one other house in the street is said to contain a similar stone.

We now make our way to the village of South Tawton, passing en route Moon's Cross already described. This is a typical Devonshire village where the church, the church house, the pub and a number of pleasant old cottages and houses cluster round an open space which, although now covered with tarmac, was once the village green.

In the centre of the square, there stands an ancient and much pollarded elm tree, surrounded by a massive plinth of granite masonry. Upon this plinth is a memorial slab which records that the wall around the tree was re-built to commemorate the Coronation of Her Majesty Queen Elizabeth II. The inscription refers to the tree as the "Cross Tree", as do all the inhabitants of South Tawton. Whether a cross ever stood here or not one cannot say, there is absolutely no evidence that this was the case. On the other hand this is just the kind of village that one would expect to have a village cross and the name Cross Tree must have some significance though of course the reference may be to the fact that four roads meet here. I have a private theory that the splendid and massive cross head at West Wyke, already described, may have come from here. But, alas, theories and evidence are different things.

However, having arrived at South Tawton, I refuse to leave before recounting a story told me many years ago with great glee by an ancient native over a pint in the Seven Stars. I suspect the story of being apocryphal, but there may be a glimmer of truth . . .

It appears that several years ago (I think it was intended to imply that the events took place in the 1930's) the powers that be decided that South Tawton was badly in need of parking space for cars. The village green was the obvious place for this but the ancient Cross Tree with its attendant masonry was in the way. A considerable and acrimonious discussion took place but at the end of the meeting, the forces of progress won the day and the edict went forth — the Cross Tree must go. A contractor was engaged and on the appointed day he arrived with a massive and powerful traction engine. The driver backed up to the tree and connected it to his engine with a stout steel chain. He then took up the strain and eased gently forward in lowest gear; the engine faltered and . . . the chain broke. The chain was repaired and the process was repeated, and again the chain broke. And so it went on, all through the long hot summer's day. When evening came the contractor had no chain left, some damage had been done to the churchyard wall and the Cross Tree stood unscathed where it had stood for centuries. "And so" said my informant "they held an emergency meeting and decided to leave the tree alone. And it's still there".

Chagford: Several crosses marking tracks or standing along lanes in the vicinity of Chagford have already been described but the town itself presents an interesting specimen for our examination which at the same time provides a puzzle which has not so far been solved. The little town of Chagford, or village as the residents prefer to call it, is one of the four ancient Stannary Towns of Devon. It is a charming place and possesses many splendid old houses and other buildings; indeed, Chagford provides a feast for the lover of atmosphere.*

The beautiful church of St. Michael stands in a large churchyard with many ancient graves. Some years ago it was found necessary to extend the churchyard and this was done by incorporating some of the adjoining ground to the north of the church. In this extension to the churchyard will be found the town's War Memorial. This consists of a tall granite cross of which no better description can be given than that of Masson Phillips published in 1937; "A restored cross, serving as a war memorial, erected in 1928. A modern pedestal of two octagonal steps, the lower with a chamfered plinth and a projecting top edge, the upper plain, supports an ancient . . . octagonal socket-stone, the sides of which are ornamented with mouldings. The socket-stone bears a modern shaft of rough rectangular section to which has been attached the upper portion of the shaft, with head and arms, of an ancient cross . . . On the face, between the arms, there is an incised cross. This cross was formerly built into a wall at Holy Street, and prior to that is said to have stood in, or near, the market-place at Chagford. The socket-stone, hollowed out to form a trough, once stood in the yard at Southmead House, and is also said to have once been in the market-place. This is possible, but the cross is quite different in character and certainly never belonged to the socket-stone."

From the extremely lucid description given verbatim above it will at once be grasped that Chagford's war memorial consists of some new material and parts of two ancient crosses. Ormerod provides a little further elucidation, for he, writing in 1874, says that Chagford formerly had two ancient crosses. One of these, the Market Cross, stood under a tree on the north side of the market-place. It was removed from there to Holy Street, just outside the town, where the head and arms and the upper part of the shaft was eventually built

---

* A recently published book *A History of Chagford* by Jane Hayter-Hames (Phillimore & Co.) 1981 is a mine of fascinating information about this lovely old town.

Cross in Chagford Churchyard.

into the roadside wall. What happened to the rest of this cross is not known. Ormerod mentions a second cross, which, he says, also once stood in the market-place. He says he saw this lying in a rubbish heap behind a barn at Waye Barton. He says that his impression was that before it was mutilated it must have been a cross far above the average of crosses in the district. He does not say whether he means in terms of elaborateness or size. When he saw it the head of the cross had been broken off and he says that it had very short arms. Ormerod tells us that the base of this cross was then (1874) in the possession of a Miss Clampitt of Chagford. It had been hollowed out and was in use as a pump trough. This base, says Ormerod, was of granite, octagonal in shape and ornamented with horizontal mouldings. Here one cannot avoid the thought that Ormerod is describing the socket-stone now forming part of the war memorial. But his description certainly does not fit the cross forming the upper part of the memorial.

Crossing says he saw the mutilated cross behind the farm buildings at Waye Barton in 1892. His description is similar to that given by Ormerod but he adds that the cross had obviously been used as a gatepost, the position of the holes drilled for this purpose indicating that the cross has been put into the ground head downward. He also comments upon the very short arms but seems to think that the reason for their shortness was that they had been purposely knocked off. Crossing also remarks that this cross was quite unlike the one that would be expected to belong to the socket-stone at Southmead House which he had also seen, and which there is no doubt is the one now forming part of the war memorial. He adds that he saw this cross again later and it had then had hinges fitted to it, with the intention of again using it as a gate-post. Whether this intention was carried out is not known. One very odd discrepancy between the accounts given by Ormerod and Crossing emerges. Ormerod says of the cross that he saw behind the barn at Waye Barton that ". . . before it was mutilated it must have been far above the average of the crosses in this district," though what he actually meant by this is not clear. Crossing says of what must surely have been the same cross; "It has the appearance of a wayside cross, and is certainly not what we should expect to find surmounting a base such as we have examined at Southmead House." Both these authorities are agreed that the missing cross had a cross incised between the arms. It would seem to be clear that somewhere, probably in the vicinity of Chagford there are parts of two ancient crosses waiting to be found.

In her book, *A History of Chagford* Miss Jane Hayter-Hames touches upon the ancient stone crosses which once existed in the town and in particular refers to the one that Ormerod and Crossing saw at Waye Barton.

Miss Hayter-Hames says in her book that this cross has now been re-erected on the common behind Waye Barton. Hoping that this new information would help solve the puzzle I recently paid a visit to Coombe Tor, a small outcrop of rock standing in enclosed land quite close to Waye Barton. That there is a cross here is indisputable, but not the ancient cross I had hoped to find. This one is fashioned in granite and stands about 8 feet tall and is of massive proportions with expanding head and arms. A splendid example of the stone-mason's craft, it bears the date 1908 and the initials M.A.L.C. I later learned that the cross was erected as a memorial to a member of the Coniam family who formerly owned the land. Enquiries to trace the ancient cross which Ormerod and Crossing described as being at Waye Barton again proved abortive — nothing seems to be known about it.

Moretonhampstead: This is another of those charming villages or small towns of which there are so many in Devon. Moreton (as it is usually known) is ancient indeed, it is probable that there was a Saxon settlement here as early as the 8th century. The place is mentioned in Domesday as Mortona and later — in the early 14th century — became one of the manors held by the Courtenays, Earls of Devon, who held it until 1900. Unfortunately, Moreton has suffered a series of disastrous fires over the centuries and these destroyed many of the more ancient buildings. Happily, enough have survived to allow the village to retain its charm and picturesque air. In particular the church is beautiful and the 17th century almshouses in Cross Street are superb.*

In such a place as this it is not surprising that we should find an interesting village cross and this is indeed the case. In Cross Street, near the almshouses and close to the south entrance to the

---

* More information about all aspects of Moretonhampstead's history can be found in *Sparrowhawk — The story of Moretonhampstead* by R. O. Heath published in 1977.

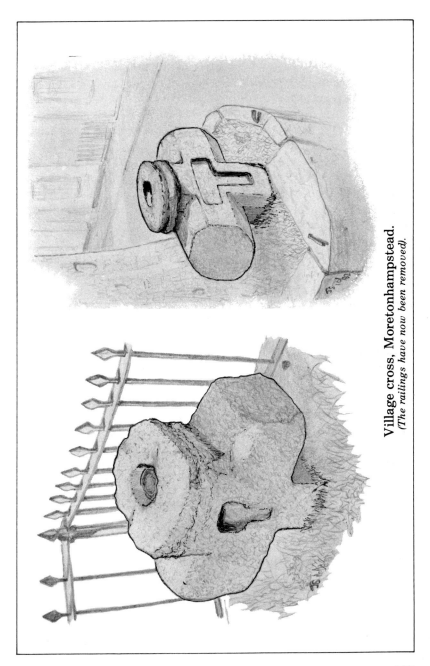

Village cross, Moretonhampstead.
(The railings have now been removed).

churchyard, we come to the "Cross Tree". This is an elm tree growing in the centre of the large and ancient pedestal which once supported the village cross. The pedestal is of stone, octagonal in shape with a projecting top edge and chamfered plinth; the various sides vary from 38 to 48 inches in length. Standing on the plinth, in front of the tree, is the upper part of the village cross. This consists of the head and arms and a very short length of the shaft. The head is octagonal in section and measures 27 inches across the arms, obviously part of a very substantial cross. The top of the head is surrounded by a moulded collar and the head has been hollowed out so as to form a cavity. The purpose of this cavity is in some doubt but two possibilities occur to me. One is that maybe the cavity was intended to serve as a stoup for holy water; the other that perhaps the head was surmounted by a finial or some other decorative feature. Between the arms, on one face of the cross, is another recess. This is shaped like a capital "T"; it is 12 inches high and 10 inches across the arms and the recess is one and a half inches deep. On the other face is a rectangular recess about 12 inches high and 4 inches wide. The precise purpose of the recesses just described seems to be unknown. My own conjecture is that they were probably intended to house images — of the Crucifixion or something similar, wrought in some material different from the granite of which the cross is formed, marble or alabaster perhaps. When the time came for the cross to be broken up or defaced, probably during the Commonwealth, it was no doubt easy enough to prise out and destroy small images of this kind. It was quite a different matter to break up a massive granite cross head and so it survived.

Ormerod, Crossing and Masson Phillips have each in turn described the Moretonhampstead cross and there is little difference in what they say, except that Masson Phillips described the cross head as standing inverted, regarding the collar around the top as marking the junction below the arms where the shaft joined the head. I do not agree with this and neither did the other two observers whose descriptions I have quoted.

In addition to what he has to say about the cross itself, Crossing devotes considerable space to a description of the function of the Cross Tree. He quotes excerpts from a private journal, dated 1800, 1801 and 1807 which describes functions held at the tree. One of these reads as follows: "August 28th. 1801. The Cross Tree, floored and seated round, with a platform, railed on each side, from the top of an adjoining garden wall to the tree, and a flight of steps in the garden for the company to ascend. After passing the platform they enter under a grand arch formed of boughs. There is sufficient room for thirty persons to sit around, and six couples to dance, besides the orchestra. From the novelty of this rural apartment it is expected much company will resort there during the summer.''

It seems that the erection of a floor for dancing etc. among the branches of the Cross Tree was a normal part of the social life of Moreton during the early years of the 19th century. Crossing tells us that he was unable to discover when the last such function was held in the tree. He says that the tree was still standing when he wrote in 1902 but that it had been very badly damaged in a storm in 1891 and was then quite hollow. It seems unlikely that the original tree survived much longer or that the present incumbent will ever be a Cross Tree in anything but name.

Throwleigh and Gidleigh: These two neighbouring Dartmoor border villages both lie to the south of the A.30 road in the vicinity of Chagford. Both have a somewhat remote air and possess extensive commons on the north-east side of the moor.

To deal with Throwleigh first. It is fortunate in still possessing what at first glance looks like an ancient village cross, occupying a position at the cross roads more or less in the centre of the village. But closer examination brings to notice an inscription on the base of the cross, which proclaims that this is a comparatively modern cross containing a very little ancient material. The inscription tells us that the cross was erected by the Rector of the parish and a parishioner to commemorate the sixtieth year of Queen Victoria's reign (1897). The only original material incorporated is the socket-stone in which the cross is fixed. As seen to-day the cross consists of a pedestal of three steps surmounted by the ancient socket-stone in which is fixed the shaft of a short modern cross of octagonal section.

Ormerod and Crossing both tell us that in the middle of the 19th century fragments of two crosses were to be seen at Throwleigh fastened together with an iron spike. Both go to some lengths in describing these fragments, one of which consisted of the head and one arm of a cross, which had a cross within a circle incised upon it. There are certain points of resemblance between this description and the mutilated cross already described, which stands on the

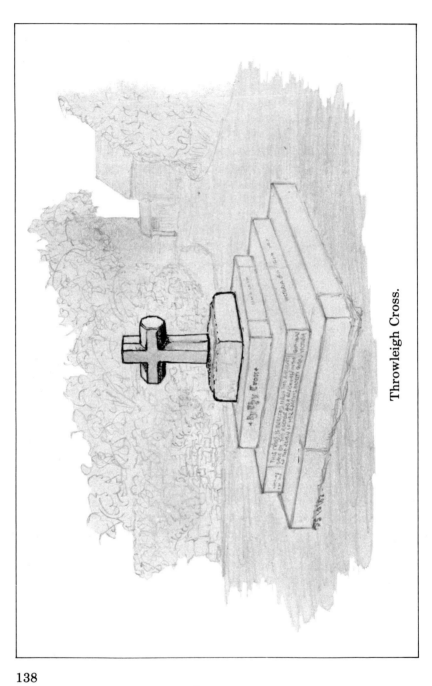

Throwleigh Cross.

roadside wall near Blackaton, about a mile from the village. However, a detailed comparison makes it fairly certain that the cross at Blackaton cannot be the fragment described by Ormerod and Crossing. If this is accepted, we are left with the certainty that yet another cross existed at Throwleigh which is missing to-day and about which we know practically nothing. Both Ormerod and Crossing desscribe the socket stone as we see it today, in which then stood the length of octagonal shaft, 2ft 9ins long, now missing.

The socket stone of the Throwleigh cross had been hollowed out and used as a trough before the restoration in 1897 and it has been filled with cement to render it serviceable in its present role. It is thought that this socket-stone once formed part of the Churchyard cross at Throwleigh.

Part of the shaft of what was once an ancient cross has recently come to light at Throwleigh. This shaft, which measures 4 feet in length overall is square at the base but chamfered above. The shaft is 11 inches by 12½ inches thick below the chamfering but reduces to 10¾ inches by 12 inches to form the tenon which fitted into the socket-stone. The shaft was found built into a wall at The Barton, Throwleigh, during recent renovations. It was brought to my attention by Mr & Mrs Hodgson, the owners of The Barton. Unfortunately there is no trace of the head of the cross to which the shaft belonged. The latter may well be part of the cross whose socket-stone stands in the centre of the village. What is to become of the newly found shaft is as yet undecided; its preservation however, is certain.

We now make for the neighbouring village of Gidleigh, which has much of interest to show. This includes, besides the ancient church, Gidleigh Castle, a fortified manor house of probable early 14th century date and the old pinfold or pound in which stray animals were confined. There is a wealth of splendid old farmhouses in the winding narrow lanes around the village.

Gidleigh has an interesting and beautiful ancient cross to show. This will be found in the churchyard, doing duty as a grave-stone on the grave of a member of the Sampson family. In the 1920's or early 1930's this cross was found, with its head buried in the ground, acting as a fencing post at Greenaway Farm just outside the village. It was removed and having been supplied with a new base by the Dartmoor Preservation Association it was re-erected near the entrance to the farm. It stood in this position for some years but was then reclaimed by the relatives of the farmer who had recently died and was used as a gravestone as we see it today. This is a fine cross with a tapering shaft, square at the base and chamfered above the stops. The head and arms expand outwards. It is in very good condition and is similar to the crosses at Hele and Addiscott, already described. Where it came from originally is unknown, it may have been a wayside cross but equally it may have been the ancient Churchyard cross removed to a place of safety until the arrival of better times. Clearly this cross is now safe from destruction but it is a pity that there is no reference to it in Gidleigh Church, either on the information sheet or elsewhere that I could find. There is a real danger that the fact that this is no ordinary gravestone will be forgotten in a few years time.

In the autumn of 1982 the present occupier of Greenaway Farm, Mrs. Weeks drew my attention to one of the gateposts of the handgate giving access to the front garden of the farmhouse. This is a massive granite post about 4½ feet tall and varying in width from about 2 feet at the base and coming to a point at the top. One side of the post has a finely worked plane surface, the opposite side undulates greatly and has a massive protuberance ending in a point. This post has all the appearance of being a stone cross in the course of construction but abandoned for some reason before completion. No information is forthcoming as to the origin of this specimen but it is clearly of considerable age. A circular hole has been bored in the post indicating its use as the pivoting point upon which a gate once swung. This type of gate construction used to be common in the Dartmoor district and is fully explained in R.H. Worth's *"Dartmoor"* pages 356/359. (Published privately 1953 but now again in print).

According to Masson Phillips an ancient cross with one arm missing used to stand in the garden of Gidleigh Castle. This cross had already disappeared when he wrote in 1937 and its present whereabouts are unknown, as is its original situation. The gatepost at Greenaway, described above, has very much the appearance of a cross with one arm missing; Is it possible that there is a connection between this and the missing cross from the castle garden?

Chapter 12

Memorial Crosses

It is proposed to devote this short chapter to the descriptions of a number of crosses which are not ancient and do not fall into any of the categories so far dealt with but which arouse comment and provoke questions from visitors.

Combe Tor, Chagford: This cross has already been referred to in the chapter dealing with churchyard and village crosses. It stands high above the surrounding countryside on the outskirts of Chagford; is in fact perched on the summit of a small tor standing in private land. The cross is a massive specimen, made from a single piece of granite and is beautifully if formally worked. It stands about eight feet tall with a tapering shaft. The head and arms expand outwards. All the edges are chamfered. The cross bears the inscription "M.A.L.C. 1908" in leaded characters. It is said to have been erected to the memory of a member of the Clampitt family, formerly the owners of the land.

Sherberton Common, Widecombe in the Moor: This cross will be found at the foot of Corndon Tor, near the road leading to Sherril and Babeny. It is a modern cross in granite, of rectangular section, standing on a plinth of dressed granite. The cross is sited upon an outcrop of rock in such a way as to make it impressive despite its modern churchyard pattern. A leaded inscription tells us that the cross was erected in memory of a member of the Cave-Penney family who was killed in the First World War. The Cave-Penneys formerly lived at Sherril, about a mile away.

The Green, Hexworthy: Here, in the tiny hamlet of Hexworthy which is more or less in the centre of the Forest of Dartmoor, will be found a massive granite cross of Cornish type with a circular perforated head. This was erected in 1897 to commemorate Queen Victoria's Diamond Jubilee. The Cornish motif is appropriate since the Forest forms part of the Duchy of Cornwall, which is in a sense a Royal Perquisite.

Brat Tor, Lydford: Brat Tor can be reached by walking along a rugged lane leading east from the Dartmoor Inn on the A.386 road. On reaching the open common the tor will be seen about three-quarters of a mile away to the east, on the further side of the valley of the River Lyd. On the summit of this conical tor will be seen Widgery Cross. A green path leads up the hillside to the tor; the path is reached by crossing the Lyd at a ford, where there are also stepping stones and a footbridge. The climb up the steep side of the tor is a stiff one but is well rewarded by the magnificent and extensive views to be obtained from the summit.

Widgery Cross, the reason for our visit to Brat Tor (also often called Widgery Tor by local people), was erected at the cost of William Widgery, a well known local artist, to commemorate the Golden Jubilee of Queen Victoria in 1887. The cross is about 13 feet tall and is constructed from roughly cut blocks of granite set upon the granite of the tor. It bears an inscription which reads: "W. Widgery, Fecit, Jubilee, V.R." Personally, I find Widgery Cross rather disappointing but this is more than compensated for by the magnificent views already referred to. This compensation can be enhanced on the return journey by returning downstream along the Lyd after crossing at the ford and following the river along for about 300 yards. This brings the walker to Black Rock, a rocky outcrop overlooking the river on its right (west) bank. Here will be found a seat commanding the valley and a plaque fixed to the rock in memory of a young officer killed in the first World War. Altogether an evocative, peaceful and beautiful spot.

Cornwood: In the centre of the village of Cornwood stands an imposing monument in the shape of a granite cross upon a stepped base. At first glance one would expect this to be the village War Memorial but in fact it turns out to be a memorial to Frederic Rogers, Baron Blachford, who died in 1902. Lord Blachford was a distinguished Civil Servant and spent his later years at Blachford, in Cornwood, where he was Squire and much loved by local people. The Barony of Blachford is now extinct.

Hand Hill, Forest of Dartmoor: On the north-western slopes of Hand Hill, not far from the headless cross described when the old Monks' Path was under discussion, a new cross has recently (1982) made its appearance. This stands upon the top of a pointed granite boulder; the cross is about 6 inches tall, made from brass or some similar metal and bears no inscription whatever. It is firmly cemented to the boulder upon which it stands. I do not know who erected this cross but suspect that it commemorates some recently deceased person whose ashes may have been scattered nearby. This may be regarded as harmless as far as it goes but it would be a pity if this practice were to proliferate.

Hameldon, Widecombe-in-the-Moor: On the higher slopes of Hameldon, above the Natsworthy valley which runs northward out of Widecombe, stands a granite monolith about six feet tall which bears an incised cross and an inscription which consists of the letters "R.A.F. S.49. 21.3.41" and four sets of initials. This is a monument to the crew of a Hampden bomber which crashed at this spot when returning from an operation over enemy territory. For anyone interested in finding this memorial, it stands on the spur just north of Berry Pound (approximate map reference 713804) and is best approached from Natsworthy Gate.

Little Sherberton or Dunnabridge, Nr. Hexworthy: This cross stands near a ford on the West Dart, opposite Little Sherberton Farm. It is on land belonging to Dunnabridge Farm. (MR 639737). The cross is of granite, roughly but carefully shaped in the typically Dartmoor idiom. It stands about five feet tall and has all the appearance of an ancient Dartmoor cross except that when carefully examined it becomes apparent that it is considerably less weathered than would be the case if it were several centuries old.

This cross is not shown on any map of Dartmoor, nor is it referred to in any of the books about the Moor that I have read. The only reference to it is in T.D.A. Vol. 111 (1979) where it is described by Mr Masson Phillips to whose notice I brought it in the 1960's.

I discovered this cross by accident about 1969, but on making enquiries of my acquaintance Mr Newman Caunter, the then tenant of Dunnabridge Farm, I found that its existence was well known to local people. Mr Caunter told me that the cross had been made by his father some 40 or 50 years earlier at the request of a Plymouth doctor, whose young son had been drowned in the river near this spot. To my mind the most interesting thing about this cross is the fact that it was made by a Dartmoor farmer from Dartmoor granite more or less in situ. This illustrates the survival of a craft in the hands of a craftsman to whose ancestors such a task was no doubt a familiar thing over many centuries.

This cross is best approached from Dunnabridge Farm. It should be noted that it stands on private land and permission to visit it should be sought at the farm.

Windy Post.

South Harton Cross.

Chapter 13

New information about some Dartmoor Crosses

Since the first edition of this book came out in 1983 there have been several developments which I am sure people who take an interest in Dartmoor crosses would like to know about. A few new finds have been made, there have been some changes in location and I have had my attention drawn to a few crosses which had previously escaped my notice. The publication of a new edition provides an opportunity to bring the record more nearly up to date and this chapter is devoted to this end. But it must be remembered that this branch of archaeology is an on-going thing with developments constantly occurring – it is impossible to claim that any record is definitive, it never will be. The following is a list of crosses, or parts of crosses, which were either not described in the first edition or, in respect of which, material developments have occurred since its publication. The sequence of individual crosses in the accompanying list has been done on a purely arbitrary basis, but in most cases map references are given to make searching easier.

Elsford Cross (Hennock) GR792829 (*): On page 90 of the first edition I commented that a cross described by both William Crossing and E.N. Masson Phillips as standing at the roadside near Elsford Farm, between Hennock and Moretonhampstead, could not now be found. This statement intrigued a friend of mine, Ernest Ilieve (now unhappily deceased), who lived not far away, and he decided to search for it himself. His efforts were rewarded, as mine had not been and he eventually discovered the cross which over the years had been covered over with roadside debris and was completely hidden from view. Ernest removed the covering and the cross, a mere remnant of what was once a massive granite monument, is now plain for all to see. The remnant consists of the head and arms (one arm is badly broken) and a short piece of the shaft. The whole thing stands about 23 inches high and is 31 inches across the arms. It is of somewhat rude construction and is typical of the kind of wayside cross we find around the Dartmoor borders. We know nothing of the age or history of this cross, but it seems pretty certain that its original position was at or near where it now stands. It probably marked the track to the churchtown – Moreton or Hennock – long before the track became a road; perhaps as early as the 13th century. The cross stands on the north side of the road, right opposite the entrance to Lower Elsford Farm.

Church House, Walkhampton (*): On page 47 is a reference to a cross shaft and socket which at the time of writing were then lying by the roadside in the lane leading to Walkhampton church. In 1984 the shaft and socket were brought together and erected opposite the ancient Church House, near where they were found. This restoration was financed by the generosity of Mrs Helen Andrew, who formerly lived nearby. It will be noticed that the socket-stone of this cross is triangular in shape and of very rough construction. I am quite sure that in its original condition the socket-stone would have been below ground level and not on view, as it is in its restored form. Sockets of this kind, where the shaft actually penetrates the socket, are fairly common in the Dartmoor district. The shaft in question is of granite and it has the remains of an iron gate or door catch embedded in it. Nothing is known of the whereabouts of the head of this cross and nothing of its original site or purpose. It may have been the churchyard cross from the nearby church or a wayside cross marking the route to the church or the monks' path to Buckland Abbey, not far away. The shaft and socket are so different in type and construction that I think it unlikely that they originally formed part of the same cross. I have seen a drawing by Samuel Prout of early 19th century date which shows quite clearly the shaft referred to forming part of a lean-to building at the eastern end of the Church House. This building has now disappeared.

Well Town, Walkhampton GR540700 (**): A tall granite shaft of rectangular section with chamfered edges was found some years ago in a nearby farm building. The shaft has now been erected by the roadside close to the farm, the work having been carried out at the instance of the Dartmoor National Park Authority. This looks like the shaft of a wayside cross, perhaps from the monks' path from Buckfast to Buckland, which runs nearby. The head is missing and its whereabouts are unknown.

Spurrell's Cross.

The Garden House, Buckland Monachorum GR498682 (**): Doing duty as a gatepost at the entrance to a cottge in the grounds of the Garden House is a rectangular granite shaft, broken off at the point where the shaft widened out to form the arms. Identity unknown but probably brought from a distance. There are numerous pieces of worked stone strewn all round the vicinity.

Shaugh Prior Churchyard (**): In *Transactions of the Devonshire Association*, Vol. LXIX (1937), page 305, E.N. Masson Phillips records the existence of an octagonal socket-stone with a square socket hole lying among the graves near the South Door of the church. Also, forming the coping of the wall beside the steps at the east entrance to the churchyard is an octagonal granite shaft about 5ft. long. It is square at one end and there are projections at the other end which seem to indicate that the shaft broke off at the point where it joined the arms. The head and arms are missing. This is probably the shaft of the ancient churchyard cross and the socket in the churchyard probably belongs to it.

The Village Green, Sourton GR533903 (**): On the green, not far from the socket-stone and stump of the old village cross, will be found a tall granite shaft decorated on two sides with circles, crosses and saltires. This shaft was found in an out-building at a nearby farm and erected here by the National Park Committee in 1985. There is a bronze plaque on a boulder close by stating this fact. The shaft has been identified as a Saxon memorial stone of the 10th century or earlier.

Cross at Sourton Down GR547917 (**): The cross which used to stand at the junction of the A30 and the A386 (see page 88) has been moved temporarily to a place of safety. It stood right at the spot where the new Okehampton bypass road meets the A386 and so would have been in some danger of damage if left where it was. It will eventually be re-erected in the vicinity of its old site – this may well have happened by the time this new edition is published. It is a particularly interesting and important cross because of its early Christian (6th century) inscription.

Okehampton Churchyard (**): New to me but recorded by E.N. Masson Phillips in *Transactions of the Devonshire Association, Vol.*

Saxon Cross, Sourton Green.

Ringhole Copse Cross.

LXIX (1937) page 333, a tall granite shaft, square at the base but octagonal above. It stands just inside the west gate of the churchyard having been found doing duty as a gatepost nearby in 1928, when it was moved to its present position and given a new head and arms. An interesting point is that the shaft is club-footed, which seems to indicate that it never had a socket stone. There is a suggestion that the cross may originally have stood at the junction of the church lane with the Hatherleigh road – as a waymark to the church perhaps.

If you go to look at the cross just mentioned do have a look at the stone grave-slab in the church porch. It has a cross incised on it and an inscription which reads HIC JACET ROBERTUS DE MOLIS. The de Molis family lived at Chichacott, close by, and it is suggested that this is the interment slab of Robert de Molis who died whilst on crusade, prior to 1233. The slab was found in 1843, after the church had been burned down.

Cross at Ringhole Copse, South Tawton GR671941: This cross stood at the spot it had occupied for centuries until 1985 or 1986 (see page 84). It has now been moved to a new position, its original site having been obliterated during the construction of a new bypass, a section of the A30. The cross now stands on the verge of the side road, overlooking the bypass quite near its old location and close to a point where a bridge for local traffic crosses the new road.

Cross on Ter Hill GR641706: This is the westernmost of the two crosses on Ter Hill (see page 34). In 1984 the cross was found to have fallen, probably knocked over by some animal using it as a rubbing post. The cross had broken in falling – it will be remembered that it had already been broken and repaired in 1885. This cross is a registered ancient monument and there was some delay in obtaining the consent of the D.o.E. for it to be repaired. This was eventually forthcoming however and the cross was taken away for repair. After an absence of some months it was brought back and re-erected. It is now in better condition than I ever remember it.

Cross Shaft at Throwleigh (**): On page 139 there is a reference to the finding of part of an ancient cross shaft at The Barton,

Ter Hill Cross.

Throwleigh. In 1985 the shaft was set up in the churchyard at Throwleigh by the National Park Authority with a bronze plaque relating its provenance.

Boundary stone on Gidleigh Common GR649891: At the east foot of Kennon Hill, marking the boundary between Gidleigh and Throwleigh parishes is a tall boundary stone, more than six feet tall. This bears the letter "G" for Gidleigh and an incised cross. See the comments on page 104, where Stittleford's Cross is dealt with, regarding the possible significance of a cross cut upon a boundary stone.

Gatepost at foot of Kingshead Lane, Widecombe GR716770: The gatepost at the latch end of the gateway leading from the Natsworthy Valley road, Widecombe, to Kingshead Farm, is a tall granite post and has an incised cross cut upon it, near the top. It seems likely that this too was once a boundary stone, now serving a second period of usefulness.

Ilsington – lane leading to Lounston Farms from Willis's Cross, Liverton GR792751: In *Transactions of the Devonshire Association*, Vol. LXVI (1984), page 143, E.N. Masson Phillips refers to a granite shaft, then in use as a gatepost, at a gateway on the south side of the road. The post has a cross incised upon it near the upper end. Since the report referred to, the post has been broken and replaced; it cannot now be found. If this stone turns up again it will be erected in the vicinity by the National Park Authority. This post has all the appearance of a boundary stone and may have belonged to one of the three manors existing within the parish of Ilsington.

Swallerton Gate, Manaton GR739791: In *Transactions of the Devonshire Association, Vol. LXII (1940)*, page 267, E.N. Masson Phillips records the presence in the grounds of the Hound Tor Inn (now known as Swallerton Gate) of the head of a cross and a short piece of shaft. There is an incised cross between the arms on one side. This fragment stands about 16ins. high overall and is about 12ins. wide. The arms are unusually short. The cross has now been built into the roadside wall of the garden at Swallerton Gate, facing the road. The house is now a private residence. Nothing is known of the history of this cross except that it was found in an adjacent hedge in 1939. Judging from its appearance I would guess that it once belonged to a wayside cross and that it was picked up from the common when someone was collecting stone for wall building.

Two Thorns Cross, Holne Moor GR677709: Recent investigations into the prehistoric and medieval settlements on Holne Moor indicate that a wayside cross probably stood on Holne Moor at a spot betwen Horns Cross and the valley of the Ventiford Brook at the point where the brook flows into the reservoir. It is thought that this cross was the easternmost marker on the monks' path from Buckfast to Buckland. The probable site of the cross is indicated by a setting of boulders perched upon a reave and the archaeologists concerned have named it "Two Thorns Cross" because of the presence nearby of two prominent thorn trees. There is some documentary evidence that the track itself was named the Maltern Way and that the name was in use in the early 17th century. It will be remembered that William Crossing was told of a belief that there was a cross, other than Horns Cross, somewhere on Holne Moor but that he was never able to find it. See *The Ancient Stone Crosses of Dartmoor and its Borderland* by William Crossing, page 103. (Devon Books, 1987). For a full account of the archaeological investigations referred to above see *Medieval Settlement and Land Use on Holne Moor, Dartmoor: the Landscape Evidence*, by Andrew Fleming and Nicholas Ralph in *Medieval Archaeology*, Vol. XXVI, (1982).

Sticklepath (near Ladywell) GR639942); and Bude Lane (GR631948): At the positions indicated stand two inscribed stones decorated in a similar manner to the one now erected on the Green at Sourton. The markings at Sticklepath however are not nearly so clear as in the Sourton specimen. Also, in the case of the stone near the Ladywell, in addition to the incised markings, one side of the stone has upon it a cross in relief of the type known in heraldry as a "cross pomel". This has a greatly extended shaft which gives it much the appearance of a sword. The original purpose and provenance of these stones is unknown but they seem at present to be acting as parish boundary markers. But if the Sourton stone is really of Saxon origin, as is supposed, I feel that these are almost certainly of the same period. For a discussion about these stones and some excellent drawings see a paper by E.N. Masson Phillips in *Transactions of the Devonshire Association*, Vol. LXIV (1987).

Brent Moor northwest of Three Barrows GR651631 (*): On Brent Moor, about 600 yards northwest of Three Barrows, is a boundary stone, one of a series marking the boundary between the parishes of South Brent and Ugborough. This stone has something of the appearance of a cross and on some of the older O.S. 1:25000 maps it is named as Hobajon's Cross. This it certainly is not. The genuine cross of this name is now represented by a boundary stone with a cross incised upon it which stands more than a mile away to the south on the Harford/Ugborough boundary. The stone near Three Barrows is not even a cross, in the proper sense of the word, in that it has never received the attentions of a mason. Its resemblance to a cross is, I believe, purely accidental. The mapmaker's mistake has been rectified on more recent maps.

Princetown – in the churchyard (*): In the churchyard at Princetown, just beyond and to the NW of the church, stands a large modern cross. The cross is of granite, of rectangular section and about ten feet tall. The cross stands in an octagonal socket which in turn is raised upon an octagonal base of three stages. Both socket-stone and base are also of granite. This monument bears no inscription whatever. It is said that the cross was made at Dartmoor Prison by prison labour in 1912 and that it was erected in memory of the many convicts who had died at the prison since its inception and who lie buried in unmarked graves. Since 1912 prisoners who die at the prison are buried in the churchyard, their graves being marked by small headstones bearing the initials of the deceased and the date of death.

Southcott, Okehampton: In the hamlet of Southcott, parish of Okehampton, a little over two miles west of the town, at GR551948. A tall and massive granite cross of octagonal section. I believe this cross to be unique in Devon in that it has a crude representation of a crucified figure between the arms on the face fronting the road. The cross is built into the garden wall of a cottage and is hard up against the hedge. Consequently the other face cannot be seen. But it is possible to insert a hand behind the unseen face and feel upon it another incised device. This is said to represent the figure of a monk with hands clasped in prayer.

The Southcott cross is described, with a good photograph, by E.N. Masson Phillips in *Transactions of the Devonshire Association, Vol. LXIX (1937), p.334.* It is not mentioned by Crossing but is referred to in *Some Account of the Barony and Town of Okehampton* by W.B. Bridges (second edition 1889, Ed. W.W.K. Wright, p.121). It is unfortunate that since Masson Phillips photographed this cross in the 1930s lichen was formed over the incised figure on the face to such an extent as to nearly obliterate it. This could easily be remedied and this is being suggested to the authorities.

Nothing is known of the history of this cross except that it was in what seems to have been its present position in the early 19th century. My guess, for what it is worth, is that the cross is probably of 13th century date or possibly earlier. I think that it was established as a waymark in the maze of lanes in the remote country west of the town. It may have had some association with the Priory of Brightley, which was founded near Okehampton Castle in 1133 to accommodate a group of Cistercian monks. The monks later moved to Ford Abbey but the priory remained, as the Chapel of Brightley, until the middle of the 16th century.

This cross is so unusual that I feel justified in including it in a book about Dartmoor crosses despite the fact that it is some little distance from the borders of the Moor, albeit in the parish of Okehampton.

Prison Enclosures, Princetown: Dartmoor explorers who find themselves walking along the footpath by the Prison Leat which flows southward through the enclosures north of the Two Bridges/ Tavistock road may come across a cross formed from three pieces of granite set in a slab of concrete laid horizontally. This is a memorial to Cyril Sinclair, a prison employee whose duty it was to look after the leat. Mr Sinclair was killed by lightning during a violent thunder storm on 6th July, 1983. The cross was made and placed in its present position by Mr Ron Joy, a colleague of Mr Sinclair. It is understood that no public right of way exists along the prison leat but a public footpath runs parallel with the leat, a little to the east.

Southcott Cross, Okehampton.

In conclusion: the frequency with which the name of Edwin Noel Masson Phillips, F.S.A. occurs in this book will not have escaped the reader. The fact is that Ted Masson Phillips was for many years by far the foremost authority on the subject of ancient stone crosses and boundary stones and waymarks in the County of Devon. He was also a notable historian, archaeologist and geologist. It is with great regret that I record that my old friend died in July, 1987, at the age of 78. He is greatly missed.

N.B. Items in the list above marked with an asterisk (*) were referred to by me for the first time in my book *Dartmoor – Then and Now*, which was first published in 1986. Items marked with a double asterisk (**) have previously been the subject of comment by me in the columns of *Dartmoor Magazine*.

APPENDIX

Some other Dartmoor Tracks

As has already been explained, William Crossing, in his *Guide to Dartmoor* lists no fewer than 81 tracks, which, to a greater or lesser extent, traverse the Moor. Many of these are little used today because they originally served only a limited local purpose. Many of them connected farms now abandoned or unoccupied, or linked farms or villages with peat-ties, which of course are no longer used.

On the other hand there are several ancient tracks still much used, if only by ramblers, because they take the explorer into remote parts of the Moor and because they have romantic associations or evocative names which lure the seeker after Darmoor lore. It seems a pity not to include a reference to some of these tracks in such a book as this, even though, strictly speaking, they do not qualify for a place in it because they are not marked by crosses. I therefore propose to give brief details of a few of the more interesting of these tracks in this Appendix in the hope that the reader will find the subject interesting and follow it up when he has exhausted his pursuit of crosses.

BLACK LANE (NORTH) This old road was used by the peat cutters of earlier days as the route which enabled them to reach the peat-ties around the source of the Walkham River with their pack horses or peat carts. The track leaves the road at Baggator Gate, north of Peter Tavy, and runs eastward, coinciding for some distance with the line of the Lich Path, about which more later. The track then veers left (north) and mounts the slopes below Lynch Tor. It does not go over the tor however, but sweeps round it to the north, and east. Beyond Lynch Tor various branches go off to the long abandoned peat diggings. One branch actually reaches the old Walkham Head peat works where the scanty ruins of various buildings can be found. If the explorer wants to experience the true remoteness of Dartmoor he cannot do better than spend a day rambling in the area served by this old track. It is also useful if Fur Tor is the goal, as it will take him to within a mile or so of the tor by a route which is a good deal easier than some.

BLACK LANE (SOUTH). This track originally served much the same purpose as its northern namesake, in that it enabled local people to drive cattle to pasture and to reach the peat-ties in the remoter parts of southern Dartmoor. At its southern end the track commences at a point where there is a ford on the Black Lane Brook (otherwise the Wollake or Dark Lake) near the spot where that stream falls into the Erme. The ford in question is where the Abbots' Way crosses the stream, en route to or from Tavistock. There are other tracks in the vicinity, coming up from Wrangaton, Harford and New Waste near Cornwood, all of which arrive at or near the ford. The great point about the Black Lane is the fact that it takes advantage of a strip of harder ground running parallel with the Black Lane Brook, near its eastern bank. In its course the track passes close to Ducks' Pool, one of the remotest places on Dartmoor. Half a mile further on the track passes the boggy spot where the stream rises and now the track becomes a shallow gully, obviously dug out by man centuries ago. This gully is followed as it veers right and then left, after which it runs into Fox Tor Gert, down which a little stream flows through the massive tinners' works below Fox Tor. The tor itself can be seen above and to the right. Beyond Fox Tor lies Fox Tor Mire, along the southern side of which runs the Monks' Path. This is reached from Fox Tor via a hunting gate in the newtake wall quite close to Childe's Tomb. No peat is carted and few cattle are driven along Black Lane today, but it is used by hundreds of walkers in search of the remoter parts of the Moor.

THE LICH PATH This was reputedly the track used by the ancient dwellers in the Forest when visiting their parish church at Lydford. Lydford was also of course the seat of the manor court and the Stannary prison, and many must have been the reasons for visiting what was then the capital of the Moor. The name, Lich Path, means literally the Path of the Dead and it is in this connection that it is best known. Most of the Ancient Tenements of the Forest lay in the area where Postbridge now stands and in the valley of the West Dart, e.g. Hexworthy, Huccaby, Dunnabridge, etc. Prior to 1260 people living in these areas, remote as they were from Lydford, had to go there for all religious purposes, including burial. In a petition addressed to the Bishop of Exeter in 1260 it was stated that some of these farms were eight miles further from Lydford than from Widecombe if the weather was fair. In foul weather (i.e. when the streams were in spate), the difference was fifteen miles. In consequence the Bishop gave the residents at some of the farms conditional permission to use Widecombe instead. Nevertheless, many if not most of them would from time to time have found it necessary to visit Lydford, and the Lich Path would then be their route.

The exact starting place of the Lich Path seems to be unknown but it probably lay somewhere in the vicinity of Bellever, where there were two tenements, with others nearby. The track went from Bellever, crossing the Cherry Brook, the West Dart, the Cowsic River, the Walkham and the Tavy at fords which can still be found. It forded the Tavy at Cataloo Steps, near Coffin Wood. This little wood is said to have got its name from the fact that here the coffin awaited the arrival of the deceased, who had been brought thus far by packhorse or litter. In the wood the body was transferred to the coffin and then carried the last three miles of its journey with greater dignity than was afforded by a packhorse. (If the river was in spate it would be crossed at Standon Steps, a little further upstream).

West of the Tavy the Lich Path passed close to Willsworthy Farm, where there was a chapel in medieval times. It then pursued a more or less north-westerly course across moorland and through enclosures, finally emerging onto what is now the A.386 road near the farm of Beardon, about a mile from Lydford Church. The last three miles or so of this ancient track are today somewhat inconclusive and discontinuous. But much of interest can be found by the explorer who attempts to piece it together and for a person in search of an enhanced knowledge of the Moor it is well worth investigating.

THE MARINERS' WAY. The track has been mentioned more than once in the preceding chapters but it is felt that a little further information about it may be of interest. In his *Guide to Dartmoor* William Crossing gives the track quite a lot of space, though not under its present name. He refers to it as "Part of an Ancient Way from Bideford to Dartmouth . . ." which, traditionally, is just what it was. It is said that in medieval times sea-faring men who had been paid off at one or other of the North Devon ports were in the habit of making their way across the county to Dartmouth, or some other port on the south coast, (or vice versa of course), in search of a new berth. In traversing the county these hardy sailors made use of the

163

Mariners' Way, which crosses the eastern side of the Moor from the vicinity of South Zeal to Widecombe in the Moor. The true line of the track north and south of Dartmoor is in some doubt and today lies almost exclusively through lanes. But the Dartmoor section can, to a large extent, still be followed and is indicated on the current 1:25000 O.S. sheets and on finger posts along the way.

Briefly the track, on leaving South Zeal on the northern edge of the Moor, sweeps round Cosdon Hill (Cawsand on the map) and makes its way through the lanes towards Throwleigh via a farm named Clannaborough. From here it went to Ford and then to Gidleigh. Passing through the village the track descends to the North Teign River by way of Gidleigh Park. It crosses the river at Glassy Steps where today there is a footbridge but where traces of the ancient ford can still be detected. Beyond the river it mounts the steep side of South Park and then goes either by Featherbed Lane or Teigncombe, where there was another medieval chapel. It then goes on to a series of ancient farms with splendid and evocative names, in some cases actually passing through the farm-yard; e.g. Great Frenchbeer, Teignworthy, Yardworthy, Higher and Lower Shapley, Hurston, Jurston and Lettaford. The track crosses the Tavistock to Moretonhampstead road (the B.3212) at Moorgate and goes on to Leeper (now renamed Moorgate) and comes to West Coombe. At this latter place the track passes through an ancient building and emerges on the other side. It has been suggested that this was the site of one of the medieval rest-houses which existed at intervals along the track and that the wayfarer not only passed through the house but perhaps spent the night there in the process. Beyond West Coombe the route goes on past (or through) Hookney, Kendon and Heathercombe farms and eventually emerges into a lane near Natsworthy Manor about 2¼ miles north of Widecombe. From this point southwards the track is lost in lanes though it is possible to work out sensible and probable routes which would bring the traveller to Dartmouth, Brixham, Paignton or Plymouth with a minimum of fatigue.

SANDY WAY. This track starts at Michelcombe, a tiny hamlet deep in the valley of the Holy Brook about a mile SW of the village of Holne. The track pursues a more or less westerly course, the first couple of miles or so of which are all up hill. Once the high ground is reached however the going is good and the views tremendous. This is a very good way of getting right into central southern Dartmoor and getting close to such remote spots as Ryders Hill and Caters Beam. Followed right through, the track brings the traveller to Princetown, though towards the western end the track is somewhat indistinct and then merges with lanes. No doubt this route was followed long ago by some of the travellers from the Ashburton district who were making their way towards Tavistock and beyond. It is also pretty certain that in the days when French and American prisoners of war were lodged at Princetown the country people from the south-eastern quadrant of the Moor went this way to attend the market at the prison.

Manaton Churchyard Cross.

Bibliography

Ormerod, G.W.	*Wayside Crosses in the district bordering the East of Dartmoor.* T.D.A. Volume VI (1873—74). This paper later reprinted and bound up with others by the same author in a volume entitled *Archaeological Memoirs Relating to the East of Dartmoor.* Published by H.S. Eland of Exeter, 1876.
Crossing, W.	*The Ancient Crosses of Dartmoor, with a description of their Surroundings,* 2nd. edition, 1887. Published by C.E. Mathews. London and J.G. Commin, Exeter. *The Old Crosses of the Dartmoor Borders.* 1892. Published by Mathews and Lane, London and J.G. Commin, Exeter.*The Ancient Stone Crosses of Dartmoor and its Borderland.* 1902. Published by J.G. Commin, Exeter. *Guide to Dartmoor.* 2nd edition, 1912. Published by The Western Morning News, Plymouth.
Bray, Anna Eliza. Mrs	*Traditions, Legends, Superstitions and Sketches of Devonshire on the Borders of the Tamar and the Tavy.* 2nd edition 1838. 3 volumes. Published by John Murray, London.
Risdon T.	*The Chorographical Description or Survey of the County of Devon.* 1811. Published by Rees and Curtis, Plymouth.
Worth R.H.	*Dartmoor,* (1953) published privately. This volume was compiled by the author's executors from some of his many writings (in T.D.A. and elsewhere) over many years. The chapter entitled *On Dartmoor Tracks and Guide-Stones* is particularly relevant. This book is now in print again, published by David & Charles, Newton Abbot.
Finberg H.P.R.	*Tavistock Abbey: a study in the Social and Economic History of Devon.* 1951, Cambridge University Press and 1969, David & Charles, Newton Abbot. *Childe's Tomb.* T.D.A. Vol. 78. (1946)
Masson Phillips, E.N.	*The Ancient Stone Crosses of Devon*: Parts I & II. T.D.A. 1937. (Vol. LXIX) and 1938 (Vol. LXX). Supplementary papers on the same subject appeared in T.D.A. volumes for 1939, 1940, 1943, 1954, 1959, 1979, 1984 and 1987.
Harding Thompson W.	*Devon — a survey of its Coasts, Moors and Rivers* 1932. Published by University of London Press for the Devon Branch of the Council for the Preservation of Rural England.
Chudleigh, John	*Devonshire Antiquities.* 2nd edition 1893. H.S. Eland, Exeter. Contains illustrations of 80 crosses etc.
N.B.	The abbreviation T.D.A. frequently used above, refers to the annual volumes of the *Reports and Transactions of the Devonshire Association.* These date from 1868 and are still in progress. These volumes will be found in the reference sections of most of the larger branches of the Devon County Libraries and are packed with fascinating information about many different aspects of the County of Devon.

The Cross Tree—South Tawton.

Index

170

Supplementary Index

Cross on Wigford Down.

Cross in Mary Tavy Churchyard.

Key to map

Numbers indicate approximate situation of crosses.

CY = Cross in churchyard.

V = In village.

W = Wayside cross or in roadside situation.

M = On moor

No.	Situation	Name or place	No.	Situation	Name or place
1.	M	Huntingdon +	31.	W	Beatland Corner
2.	M	Petre's +	32.	V	Shaugh Prior
3.	W	Marchants' +	33.	W	Shaden Moor
4.	M	Nuns' +	34.	W	Blackaton +
		(Siward's +)	35.	W	Entrance to Chol-
5.	M	Windypost			wich Town Farm
		(Beckamoor +)	36.	W.	Hanger Farm
6.	M	Pixies' +			Cornwood
7.	M	Whitchurch Down	37.	M	Wigford Down
8.	Abbey	Buckfast Abbey	38.	W	Greenwell Girt.
	grounds		39.	M	Urgles
9.	do.	do.	40.	M	Huckworthy
10.	W	Hawson +			Common
11.	CY	Holne churchyard	41.	V	Sampford Spiney
12.	CY	do.	42.	M	Spurrell's +
13.	M	Horns +	43.	CY	Harford Church
14.	M	Skir Hill	44.	W	Beetor +
15.	M	Down Ridge	45.	W	Moorgate
16.	M	Ter Hill			(Leeper +)
17.	M	Ter Hill	46.	W	Bennet's +
18.	M	Mount Misery	47.	V	Lustleigh
		(Fox Tor newtake)	48.	V	do.
19.	M	Childe's Tomb.			(Bishop's Stone)
20.	M	Goldsmith's +	49.	W	Higher Combe
		(Fox Tor newtake)	50.	W	Sanduck +
21.	M	Wheal Anne	51.	W	South Harton Fm
		Bottom	52.	W	Horsepit +
22.	M	Walkhampton	53.	V	North Bovey
		Common (by	54.	W	Hele +
		Devonport Leat)	55.	W	Short +
23.	M	Walkhampton	56.	W & M	Week Down
		Common	57.	W	nr Leigh Bridge
24.	M	Crazywell +	58.	W	Teigncombe
25.	W	? Leathertor +	59.	W	Blackaton nr
		(Crossgate)			Throwleigh
26.	W	Yennadon +	60.	W	West Wyke
27.	W	Lane near Walk-	61.	W	West Wyke
		hampton Church	62.	—	Gatepost at Gidleigh
28.	W	Torry Brook,	63.	W	Addiscott
		Plympton St	64.	W	Ringhole Copse
		Mary	65.	W	Oxenham +
29.	W	Browney +	66.	W	Between 64 & 65
30.	W	Truelove, Shaugh			
		Prior			

No.	Situation	Name or place
67.	—	Cross Tree, Sth Tawton
68.	W	Moons' +
69.	W	Fitz's Well
70.	W	Sourton Down
71.	V	Sourton Green
72.	V	Moretonhampstead
73.	W	Linscott +
74.	W	Headless +
75.	W	South of Fingle Bridge
76.	W	Budleigh Bridge
77.	W	Bovey Stone
78.	V	Bovey Tracey
79.	CY	do.
80.	W	Challabrook Lane Bovey Tracey
81.	W	Ouldsbroom +
82.	M	Sherberton Common
83.	W	Drywells
84.	M	Hameldon +
85.	W	Stittleford's +
86.	M	Rippon Tor
87.	V	Widecombe in the Moor
88.	CY	do.
89.	CY	Manaton
90.	CY	Buckland in the Moor
91.	W	do.
92.	W	St. Gudula's + Ashburton
93.	CY	Buckfastleigh
94.	W	Wrangaton
95.	V	South Zeal
96.	V	Throwleigh
97.	CY	Gidleigh
98.	W	Cox Tor Farm Peter Tavy
99.	CY	Peter Tavy
100.	CY	Mary Tavy
101.	M	Brat Tor
102.	V	Bickleigh
103.	W	do.
104.	CY	Buckland Mona chorum
105.	V	Sheepstor
106.	CY	Sheepstor
107.	W	Walkhampton (Entrance to Burham Farm)
108.	W	Dunstone +
109.	V	Cornwood
110.	V	Hexworthy
111.	—	Little Sherberton